YOUR FIRST FIX AND FLIP

YOUR FIRST FIX AND FLIP

INSIDER SECRETS AND A PROVEN FORMULA TO GET YOU STARTED ON YOUR FIRST FIX AND FLIP TODAY!

JEFFERY A. HAMMERBERG, CPC

HPP

HAMMER PRESS PUBLICATION
Denver - Palm Springs

Published by Hammer Press Publications
Denver, CO | Palm Springs, CA

www.FixandFlip.com

For ordering information or special discounts for bulk purchases, please contact Hammer Press Publications at 303.378.5526.

ISBN 978-0-692-08405-2
1. Business. 2. Real Estate

Printed in the United States of America
First Edition

YOUR FIRST FIX AND FLIP

INSIDER SECRETS AND A PROVEN FORMULA TO GET YOU STARTED ON YOUR FIRST FIX AND FLIP TODAY!

JEFFERY A. HAMMERBERG, CPC

HPP

HAMMER PRESS PUBLICATION
Denver - Palm Springs

Published by Hammer Press Publications
Denver, CO | Palm Springs, CA

www.FixandFlip.com

For ordering information or special discounts for bulk purchases, please contact Hammer Press Publications at 303.378.5526.

ISBN 978-0-692-08405-2
1. Business. 2. Real Estate

Printed in the United States of America
First Edition

TABLE OF CONTENTS

CHAPTER SEVEN

ACKNOWLEDGMENTS

Much appreciation to my Mastermind partner and friend Douglas Carlson, President of Carlson Mortgage for the example he sets, and the encouragement and support he has provided me on my journey over the past many years.

FROM THE AUTHOR

This is not a boring, theoretical business book. What you'll find within these pages is a concise, but fully detailed and step-by-step process for successfully completing your first buy, fix, and flip.

It's my hope, and belief, that this guide will give you the confidence to make your first real estate purchase for the purpose of fixing and flipping it at a profit!

The information herein is presented in bite-sized nuggets that you can take your time exploring, or even devour in a single sitting if you're so motivated.

My goal is to ensure you understand the essential basics of the fix and flip business, while knowing how to avoid costly mistakes.

This book is succinct, focusing on the core information of fix and flips, and provides you a quick reference that you can easily refer to during the fix and flip process.

> Use this book as your working manual during your first fix and flip. Dig in, highlight, underline, and take notes!

When it comes to realizing your financial goals, this book may well become the most useful book in your library!

Here's to your success!

—Jeff Hammerberg

PREFACE

My name is Jeff Hammerberg and I've been in real estate, in one form or another, since 1981. In addition to this book, I've authored *Beyond Not Finishing High School: 7 Simple Steps to Live the Life of Your Dreams*, a series of *MEVA self-help* informational booklets, hundreds of real estate related published articles, and a children's book called *Aerial, the Bridge with a Heart*.

I'm a real estate broker, certified personal coach, public speaker, and the founder of FixandFlip.com, an education and training source for those interested in entering the fix and flip business and beyond. I'm dedicated to using my experience and know how to help *you* succeed in the lucrative business of fixing and flipping houses.

Prior to beginning in the fix and flip industry, I had a successful career at Bell Canada Enterprise Development (BCED)—a large international commercial real estate developer. Serving many roles including; Dock master, Director of Security, Retail Manager, and Operations. Later, I served as the Director of Asset Management for the Linpro Company, a national real estate developer. As a real estate agent at Re/Max, I earned membership in their prestigious '100% Club', for agents with exceptionally high average commission levels. I was one of their top-producing professionals, and in the top one percent of real estate agents in the nation.

I eventually purchased a residential real estate office. Metro Brokers Cherry Creek, in Denver, CO and built it from a six-agent office, to a highly successful seventy-agent office, before selling the company in 2005.

My personal fix and flip journey began in 1995 when, as a real estate broker, I represented the largest fix and flip investor in Denver, Colorado. During that time, I scouted properties, evaluated deals, analyzed back-end profits, and wrote multiple offers each month. I learned a lot, gained an immense amount of invaluable experience, and eventually entered the fix and flip business myself, as a buyer and fix and flip investor!

With my own company, I initially focused on single-family homes and eventually expanded my expertise to incorporate other real estate opportunities. The properties I found particularly interesting were those known as "change of use" properties.

Years into my fix and flip journey, I started to focus more on buying income properties, multi-unit buildings, directly from owners and converted them to condominiums. This allowed each unit/apartment to be sold to individual buyers, earning me a much better rate of return than if the property had remained a traditional apartment building.

I learned to legally split duplexes for similar purposes and learned other forms of property repurposing—all of which have their own specific and intricate legal processes.

After carefully assembling a competent team including a real estate agent, a surveyor, an attorney, and multiple contractors and sub-contractors, I renovated and converted just about every type of property imaginable.

I have been directly or indirectly involved in the fix and flip process with hundreds of properties throughout my career and I want to show you how you can be successful doing the same.

It's one of my greatest pleasures to introduce people to the world of fix and flips and share my expertise and knowledge that they may benefit from it as I have. I recognize the enormous impact this business can have in changing a person's life–good market or bad, there is lots of money to be made, not to mention improving homes, neighborhoods and communities nationwide.

You can work forty hours or more each week at a J-O-B, or, you can make the equivalent of an annual salary in just one fix and flip!

In *Your First Fix and Flip*, I will cut to the chase, provide you with the information you must know now to succeed in the fix and flip business, and how to apply it. You'll have a direct, easy to follow blueprint for flipping houses, a step-by-step process from purchase to profitable sale!

Like any worthwhile destination, success in the fix and flip business is found with a roadmap, a specific process—not a shotgun approach. That is what you'll find in this book.

Success in the fix and flip business is achieved through a carefully orchestrated process—learning and using a specific formula. That's what this book provides. But you have to want it and you have to be ready. Starting a business is a big decision. This can't be a hobby. Businesses that are run like hobbies pay like hobbies.

A process precedes all successful fix and flips. Skip the process – skip the benefits and risk losing your shirt!

The key to achieving success in the fix and flip business is to work the process step by step. You might have heard the saying;

How do you eat an elephant? ***One bite at a time.***

> With a typical J-O-B, you have limited leverage and limited control. You're exchanging your time (your life) for money. There is certainly nothing wrong with having a job, if you love what you're doing. My preference is to not just be part of the team, not just run the show for someone else—I want to own it! I've decided if I'm going to be creating wealth for anyone, it will be me.

Money isn't everything—but money buys me freedom
- Money buys the freedom to make a difference in the world.
- Money buys the freedom to help my family and others.
- Money buys the freedom to do what I love.
- Money buys the freedom to travel and explore.
- Money buys the freedom to relieve worry.
- Money buys the freedom to not punch a time clock.

I have freedom! I wake up in the morning and do what I want to do. I have the time and the means to pursue my dreams. I want to show you a way to have the same!

Following my process generates results that, to others, appear to be lucky breaks.

> *"I'M A GREAT BELIEVER IN LUCK, AND I FIND THE*
> *HARDER I WORK THE LUCKIER I GET"*
> —Thomas Jefferson

In these pages, in addition to finding, fixing and flipping, I'll talk to you about building up a rental portfolio as a part of your fix and flip business.

Over the years I've held some of the fix and flip properties I've purchased and turned them into rentals. As time passes, the tenants pay off my mortgages. I can be hiking in my home state of Colorado, or in beautiful Palm Springs, California where I spend my winters, and each month, the funds from rent checks are automatically deposited into my bank account. My time is completely detached from this income source. It's passive income!

Sitting, thinking, and contemplating never made anyone rich. Without consistent action—taking the steps necessary to reach your goal, nothing happens. Nothing can change until you do.

Don't worry about deviating from the social norm. The social norm is two missed paychecks away from being broke.

What are you spending your time doing? Watching television, playing video games, surfing the web? Value your time poorly, and you'll be poor. **Engage purposefully in activities that allow you to begin laying the groundwork for beginning and growing your own business.**

If the idea of working hard to build a new business sounds daunting, how does the idea of "punching the clock" for the next twenty or thirty years sound?

There's a lot to be done to get you from where you are now, to being a success in the fix and flip business, but again—One bite at a time!

Let's get started!

YOUR FIRST FIX AND FLIP

CHAPTER ONE

ABOUT THE FIX AND FLIP BUSINESS

In this chapter, I'll give you an overview of the skills and the mindset you need to succeed in residential real estate flipping. You'll begin to discover the work ethic necessary to achieve your goals in the fix and flip business. I'll teach you about the opportunities available to newcomers in residential real estate flipping and what you'll need to get started. Finally, you'll learn about the timeline for flips and how to deal effectively with your competition.

To be a successful flipper.

In the fix and flip business it's important to realize that fixing and flipping houses *is* a business. Like any business, if you want to be successful, you must *work* the business like a business, not like a hobby. There are also some important points to keep in mind:

- You must be committed and disciplined! Cream rises to the top. Like anything in life, you get out of the business (money, freedom, opportunity), what you put into the business (time, passion, commitment).

"THERE ARE NO SECRETS TO SUCCESS. IT'S THE RESULT OF
PREPARATION, HARD WORK, AND LEARNING FROM FAILURE."
—Colin Powell

You have the advantage of learning from my mistakes and failures!

- You must be willing to work harder than anyone else would ever expect you to work. The top twenty percent of people in *any* business or company are not smarter, better looking, more connected, or luckier than anyone else. They do, however, *work harder* than anyone else.
- You must have a plan, and you must follow it. The good news is; you don't need to reinvent the wheel. The surest path to success in any field is to find someone who has mastered the business, and simply do what they did. I'm that guy for you!
- You must develop a team made up of successful, high-functioning professionals. This includes real estate agents, contractors, sub-contractors, attorneys, surveyors, assistants, etc. Your business will only be as strong as your weakest link. Hire or partner with only the most reliable, trustworthy professionals, and learn to quickly cut-ties with those that don't fit this criteria.
- You must constantly be farming for the next project. The lifeblood of your business is the next fix and flip property! If you don't reinvest your gains, your business will stall. These peaks and valleys can be the biggest challenge of starting out in the fix and flip business. You, and only you, control your destiny!

In *Your First Fix and Flip*, we'll examine each stage of the fix and flip process and what each entail. The goal of this approach is to arm you with the necessary knowledge and tools to achieve your goal of finding, fixing, and flipping a house at a profit.

That alone is a worthwhile goal, but the fix and flip business can provide even more than that. You'll also be adding value to homes, neighborhoods, and communities. In a way, you'll actively be making your city better, one house at a time! Redeveloping neighborhoods enhances the community at large.

Fixing and flipping houses can have an impact on many, not just the one who does the fixing and flipping. Renovating a home and helping to provide an improved lifestyle for the buyer has advantages for the entire community. People want to feel good about where they live and how they live. As fix and flip developers, we help people achieve that goal, while at the same time, achieving our own!

As you move into the process of owning your own fix and flip business / becoming an independent fix and flip developer, here's a few points;

1. Exceptional results require exceptional effort consisting of daily habits, routines and sacrifices; are you willing and able to bring change and new positive habits into your life?

2. The skills necessary to move into and be highly successful in the fix and flip business can be learned and mastered no matter where you currently are in life.

3. Small changes and success habits can make a huge difference in your life. The tiniest change made day after day can have a huge positive effect in your life.

> *"SUCCESS OCCURS WHEN YOUR DREAMS GET BIGGER*
> *THEN YOUR EXCUSES."*
> —Unknown

When I was in the United States Navy I worked on the bridge in the navigation department—part of my job was tracking the exact position of the ship when underway. When it was determined we were off course, an adjustment was made "Helmsman, come left one degree to…" the Helmsman would answer "Aye sir, come left one degree to…" The tiniest movement, just this one degree of difference would vastly change the ultimate destination of the ship by thousands of miles! The same is true for us, just one slight change today, just one small movement—can radically change our ultimate destination… where are *you* headed and are you willing to adjust, even one degree?

What are the opportunities in the fix and flip business?

Opportunities abound in the fix and flip business. Obviously, you can make money flipping homes, but you can also make money as a bird dog, or wholesaling properties, building a rental portfolio, adding client remodels to the mix, and more.

The fix and flip business offers a number of ways to earn revenue. Your primary focus should be on buying, fixing, and selling homes—that is where the real money is.

If you don't have the cash or the confidence to get started with your first fix and flip, there is always the *Bird Dog*, or *Wholesaler* approach, which takes zero cash, zero credit, and you can earn a few thousand, or more, per deal.

THE BIRD-DOG.

Bird Dogs are individuals that find fix and flip properties and present them to fix and flip developers. You bring the deal, and the fix and flip developer simply assumes your contract to purchase the home. When you sign a contract to purchase a home in your name, that deal will typically be written to include your "assigns," which allows you the opportunity to assign the contract to a new buyer, prior to closing. You'll want to check with your real estate agent or a real estate attorney about the specifics of this type of transaction in your state.

Here's what this scenario could look like. You've found a home and have evaluated that after investing $50,000 to fix it up, the After-Repair-Value (ARV) will be around $325,000. You agree to purchase the home for $185,000 and agree to assign the contract to a fix and flip developer for $193,000. You just netted yourself $8,000 and left room for the fix and flip developer to earn a healthy profit as well. This is a great way to begin earning cash to purchase your first fix and flip!

People who act as bird dogs are learning invaluable marketing skills. They are learning how to implement several different low-cost marketing methods that bring deals to them. They are learning how to diplomatically approach a homeowner and get the house under contract. They are learning how to value the house either by themselves or using and agent to run comparables. They are also learning how to estimate repair costs and after repair value. All of those skills are huge, putting you at least 50% of the way to becoming a fix and flip developer.

Once a bird dog really masters all these skills, he or she can leave their J–O–B and go full time into flipping. Being a bird dog is a little underrated because it's great "on the job training." You've just got very busy evenings and weekends.

Your ultimate goal should always be to become a fix and flip investor/contractor and not settle for a small piece of a deal. But I always say, "A piece of something is better than all of nothing." It's okay to begin with a small piece, as a way to get you in the game.

WHOLESALER.

Wholesalers are much like bird dogs but are typically organizations. Teams of individuals working with banks, credit unions, foreclosure attorneys, estate attorneys, etc. that have large portfolios of properties to liquidate.

If you're interested in the wholesaler route, you could form a business entity, have some business cards printed up, and make a strategic list of contacts. Swing by their offices on a Saturday morning, assuming you're still working your 9-5 job.

You could also create a target list of people like estate attorneys and bankers, send them a letter of introduction along with a business card, and swing by for a very quick in person visit.

What should you say trying to make new professional contacts? "I buy houses" is a little cheesy. What you need is a really quick elevator speech such as, "I renovate outdated homes to revitalize Denver neighborhoods" (adding your city name), or something similar.

Depending on the state of the real estate economy—their inventory may be limited, or it may be flush. Even in the Denver, CO market today, a market that I've spent my career in, there are many wholesale properties available weekly, and this is in one of the hottest markets in the nation.

If you're well organized and have the contacts to get started—wholesaling is another great avenue.

BUILDING A RENTAL PORTFOLIO.

Some of the richest people I know have made their money in real estate and no longer need to work. Most of them have done so by accumulating properties over the years. Why wouldn't you do the same? Real estate investing is the business you're trying to enter after all.

If property values are at an all-time high and you think that it's possible that they may be headed down, then it would make more sense to flip the property rather than rent it and sit around waiting for it to appreciate, because it might NOT. With some rentals, you've got people waiting in line to rent them and the rents are always nice and high, but that sort of intuition comes with time and experience.

I love driving by my brick and mortar investments and knowing the rent checks from them are being automatically deposited into my bank account each month. It's others building equity for me!

You want to collect rent, not pay rent. You want to hire employees, not be an employee. You want to lead the pack, not follow the pack.

That's part of why the fix and flip business is compelling. *You* control your destiny, not your boss, not your company, nobody—just you!

Part of owning properties is property management—another subject for another book but educate yourself on the risks and benefits of hiring this function out or doing it yourself.

Your goal should not to be to earn more and more money to support ever-increasing expenses, but to become debt-free and begin living the life of your dreams—not being nagged by the constant need for another deal.

When you come across a great property that is really undervalued, which will happen every so often, you might consider the "rental renovation" approach. A rental renovation is less involved than a total gut and remodel. You may then refinance the property (easily because it's now worth more than when you purchased it), and rent it out, thus earning money while maintaining the property in your portfolio.

Homes in Denver's real estate market have increased in value every year since I began working in the industry there, in 1991. In the city's core, homes didn't even decrease in value during the 2008 recession. Things were flat for a while, but nothing lost value. Since that time, housing values in Denver are up about fifty percent!

CLIENT REMODELS.

As you gain experience as a residential flipper, people will come to admire your work and your style. You may be approached by people who would like for you to rehab a property for them and, if you've got the time in your schedule and the money is right, go for it. Maybe your banker or attorney wants you to renovate a house?

Once you have your team established it's quite easy and profitable to add client projects into the mix. Your focus should always be finding, fixing and flipping your own projects, that's where the big money is at.

But if you're between projects, pick up a client remodel!

The one word of caution is that with client remodels, "the client" (including possibly the clients spouse, partner, financial advisor, business manager, architect …) control your schedule, not you. It can be quite frustrating to wait for "this approval," or wait for "that partners changes," etc. So, choose your client projects carefully!

What experience do I need?

To enter the fix and flip business, you do not need a college degree, or even a high school diploma! You don't need experience as a contractor, and you don't need to be familiar with the real estate industry. You don't need to be wealthy to get started, and you don't need any specialized skills.

What you do need is an ardent desire to be successful. You need to be a self-starter and self-motivated! If you're not motivated by money, if you're not motivated by the idea of working for yourself if you're not motivated by controlling your destiny—it may not be for you.

You need a sense of responsibility and organization. After all, the responsibility for the project and its positive completion will fall on your shoulders alone. Yet, you're not doing it completely alone. You'll bring with you, a team of professionals you've assembled to help ensure your success.

> *"YOUR LIFE DOESN'T GET BETTER BY CHANCE,*
> *IT GETS BETTER BY CHOICE."*
> —Jim Rohn

If you enjoy the process of taking something that needs repair and turning it into something beautiful, you're already part of the way down the road to success.

If you're a diligent, hard worker who cares about the job you do, can create and follow a schedule, and have good organization and people skills, you're well suited for the fix and flip business.

When you're looking at a run-down house and trying to visualize the end result of your renovations, possessing imagination and vision will also help immeasurably. If you can imagine what the house might look like after your redevelopment, then roll up your sleeves and let's get started! You just might be a natural-born flipper!

Where do I get the money to start?

The late-night TV charlatans hawking their get-rich-quick real estate schemes to the sleepless always distresses me. There's one thing I'd like to tell you. In most of the country you won't find "No Money Down" deals. If you do find one, chances are the property won't work as a fix and flip because it's either greatly overpriced, or it exists in such a depressed market you'll never resell it.

Forget the tricks and schemes! Go with the tried and true!

In financing a fix and flip purchase, I always use hard money lenders, where you typically need a minimum of ten percent down as a down payment. On a $150,000.00 home, you'll need $15,000.00.

You may also acquire a Federal Housing Administration (FHA) loan that requires three to five percent down, as long as the home is going to be your primary residence.

If you're a United States veteran, you can buy a house with zero down by way of a VA loan. Again, this applies only as long as the home will be your primary residence.

In a hot real estate market there are plenty of cash-buyers, and you'll have to compete with them in some cases. Rarely do VA or FHA loan buyers win a bidding process going up against cash buyers.

If you don't have the required cash on hand for the down payment, there are ways of finding it. Check out your retirement fund and see what you have available. Borrowing from your whole life insurance policy is another great option and it doesn't really compromise the death benefit.

Many people choose to go with loans from family members, but this also may mean that you have your mother, father-in-law, or uncle micromanaging your project. That's a crucial point to consider.

INSIDER SECRET: *Your ten percent cash down financing could be cash or equity in another property as security! How about a piece of jewelry, a car, boat or something else of value you own free and clear? You don't necessarily need cold hard cash.*

Scratch, beg, borrow or do whatever is (legally) necessary to get that first loan! Once the first flip is successfully sold and your loan is paid off, you're on your way, and you'll have the lender begging to loan you more.

If you can't do it alone, consider a partner (a friend or a parent) in your first project. Crowd funding and profit sharing are all great resources that can provide an entryway into the fix and flip business.

> *"IF YOU ARE BORN RICH, IT'S NOT YOUR FAULT.*
> *BUT IF YOU DIE POOR, IT'S YOUR FAULT."*
> —Bill Gates

HARD MONEY LENDERS.

Hard money lenders are great because the good ones will hold your feet to the fire, only releasing fix-up money after you have completed each stage of improvement. Again, they normally require ten percent down.

Hard money can be expensive, especially in a hot market when everyone needs money. I used to pay three points and one percent per month. Today, in a much hotter market, I pay two percent for month one, two percent for month two, and one and a half percent per month for months three through twelve. A balloon payment is due in a year.

I'm sure you'll say, "Yikes! No way would I pay that!" But you can, and your project analysis will determine that. Plus, can you imagine the negotiating power you'd have in a "cash offer" that can close in a week?

Also, you must consider the alternative issues of dealing with a bank or credit union. You could spend weeks in the approval and appraisal process, and risk losing the deal entirely at the very end prior to closing if you're not approved. Ouch!

I shoot for a fix and flip timeframe of 120 days from purchase to sale. This keeps the cost of hard money down, and keeps you motivated to finish the project. Of course, not all deadlines are met, but if you keep on track, ninety to 120 days is a reasonable timeframe to fix and flip most houses.

Another advantage to hard money lenders is they are no strangers to working with those that may be "credit challenged" if you need help in that regard. Whether or not your credit is great, if you're about to embark on your first fix and flip, there are hard money lenders ready, willing, and able to help.

OWNER-OCCUPANT THREE-PERCENT-DOWN LOAN.
When I first started fixing and flipping, I'd buy a home, fix it up over an extended period of time, and sell it after two years (tax free) then reinvest in another property. You can still do that with the new tax plan of 2018.

So, you as an owner occupy a house and fix it up. Then, keeping the tax laws in mind, you sell it and pay no capital gains! This is a FABULOUS way for a newbie to get started rehabbing. You can keep your J– O–B, for the time being, and fix up your current project in the evenings and weekends. Or you can use this strategy AND be a bird dog on the side.

Things are different for me today, but at first, I didn't have the money to own my current home *and* buy another, so my "current project" was always my principle residence. My one-hundred-and-ten-pound Giant Schnauzer, Berkeley would sometimes be her natural, beautiful black color, and sometimes a lovely shade of drywall dust!

INVESTOR REHAB LENDERS.
There are institutional lenders that specialize in providing loans to fix and flip investors. Merchants Mortgage and Trust Corporation, a lender in Denver that has been around as long as I've been in the business, gives both "fix and flip loans" and "fix and hold loans." They will lend you up to ninety percent of your purchase

price and ninety percent of your fix-up costs. In addition, if you have equity in another property, like your own home, they're happy to use that equity as opposed to requiring you to have cash on the table.

To find an institutional lender that is doing fix-up loans in your city, pull out the yellow pad and call a few banks, if they're not doing them they may refer you to someone that is. Also, don't forget to ask your real estate agent for these types of referrals.

The great majority of deals I've done have been funded by hard money lenders. I've been working with one gentleman so long that he finances one hundred percent of the purchase price. I pay for one hundred percent of the rehab costs, all the while collecting miles by using my Southwest Airlines business card for the renovation costs. As a result, I never pay to fly!

How much money can I make?

Maybe the questions should be, how hard are you willing to work? What are you willing to sacrifice in order to obtain wealth? How motivated are you to reach the point that you can quit your job and provide everything you and your family desire?

Let's look at the facts regarding the fix and flip business.

Fortune.com published an article in 2017 that cited research done by Realty Trac. According to their reports, over six and half percent of all single-family homes and condo sales were flips. This number is twenty percent higher compare to the previous quarter.

People are really catching on to flipping houses. They find it works and that it's a way to change their lives for the better. The work is both positive and rewarding. You can't keep a good thing secret for long and the statistics show flippers are becoming more numerous.

"THE BEST THING IN THE WORLD IS TO GET PAID
TO DO WHAT WE LOVE."
—Unknown

The average return on gross profits from sales of flips has been strong. The first-quarter gross profits of 2017 were listed at $58,520. That hit a ten-year high!

It's the opinion of Realty Trac senior Vice President, Daren Bloomquist that reality TV shows that covered flipping were the reason for the popularity of flipping. That may be true, but here's my opinion on some of those shows:

Many shows are guilty of making the fix and flip process seem easier than it is. Yes, they show the challenges, but it always has a happy ending.

I watched a fix and flip show rerun on Amazon recently and found it to be absolutely ridiculous! The guy they featured went over budget on almost every single step in the remodel/renovation process. In the end, he had well over $800K invested in the property, and he sold it for mid to upper $900's and exclaimed, *"Not bad. I made ninety grand on this deal. Time to find my next flip!"*

Ridiculous! By the time this guy paid the minimum in real estate commissions, he couldn't have made more than twenty grand for months of demanding work, the extreme risk that comes along with deals that involve that amount of money, not to mention the blood, sweat, and tears + time is money.

His was a failed fix and flip, and I can guess why this particular show only lasted one season. You see this scenario repeat itself.

Now not all these shows are bad, and many of them are great education, they do illustrate how unexpected things happen, and how hard it can be. You can learn helpful things from these shows. Just keep in mind, they are produced for entertainment value. Viewers are not being provided the whole story.

The truth is that if you stick to the formula set out in this book, you'll have a much better chance of success. Remember that those shows, although fun to watch, are made for entertainment purposes and offer only a snapshot of the full story. Following their pattern won't help you realize maximum profits.

How long does the fix-and-flip process take?

Give yourself a minimum of thirty days for a simple paint and carpet job. Of course, this "minimal work" will equal "minimal profits."

Remember—you'll have a period of time, from the moment you have an accepted contract, to the point of actual closing. This gives you the time you need to analyze the property and project, order materials, coordinate with and schedule your contractor and sub-contractors, etc. It's important that upon closing, you hit the ground running!

How long the process takes really depends on what kind of property you want to buy, and the condition it's in. Condominiums are generally relatively easy; you have paint, carpet, appliances and new countertops with minimum work, but also in most instances, minimum return.

Condos have the most risk, primarily because, if the real estate market gets shaky, they lose market value first. Additionally, there may be buyer loan restrictions on condominium properties—check with your real estate agent.

Also keep in mind with condos that you may have to coordinate and get approval from the home owners association (HOA) for any construction in the unit / shutting off water to install new fixtures / scheduling the elevator, etc.

A good starting point is finding a single-family home. Single-family homes are the hottest commodity! For a first-time flipper, the single-family home offers real advantages. Although they may involve more work than a condo, they're a safer investment. 90% of my fix and flips have been on single family homes.

Should I worry about competitors?

No. Competition is always healthy. There will really only be one or two individuals that will be willing to work as hard as you do, and these competitors may even become your allies. Over the years, you might buy a deal from them that they are too busy to complete, and you might sell them one for the same reason. Those that aren't working as hard as you are will never be able to compete with you.

Nobody knows the fix and flip business like those that are actually in it, so be friendly. Offer your assistance when it makes sense, and they'll be more likely to do the same.

When working with a realtor on finding a fix and flip property (my least favorite way of finding deals), chances are you'll have competitors looking at the same deals. In my market, Denver, CO, you may have thirty or more competitors, but in smaller and less hot markets, you may only have a few. You'll win a few and you'll lose many. Some you'll pass on intentionally. Don't worry about a property that you've lost—another one is on the horizon.

If you continuously compete with others, you become bitter. But if you continuously compete with yourself, you become better! If you want to stay ahead of your competitors, finding homes that are not yet listed with a real estate agent is a must.

> *"COMPETITORS PUSH YOU TO ACHIEVE MORE."*
> —M. Cobonli

Is it sustainable? Can I quit my job?

That will ultimately be up to you. But yes, if you treat your fix and flip business like a job, you can eventually quit the one you have now. I'm talking about working at least eight hours each day in your new fix and flip business. You give that to your current boss, why wouldn't you give it to yourself?

*"DO WHAT YOU HAVE TO DO, UNTIL YOU
CAN DO WHAT YOU WANT TO DO."*
—Oprah

I had an individual flip that took eight months to complete—it netted me $250,000.00 before taxes. Could you live on that? There are twelve months in the year, so how many more deals can you do, and how much more money could you make?

We've already talked about average returns in the fix and flip business. Again, in 2017 the national statistical averages are $58,520. Let's use that number and do the math to determine how many flips you need to hand in your resignation letter.

Here's the formula. Your annual income $_____ ÷ 58,520 = _____ . This is how many homes you need to find, fix & flip each year (pre-tax), to replace your current income.

Not for the faint of heart.

Despite the benefits, fixing and flipping houses is not for the faint of heart. You must be willing to tackle problems head-on and know when you need to call in reinforcements. Challenges arise on *every* job. That doesn't mean that they can't be handled. If you do your research, you'll be well prepared.

It's necessary to have a stick-to-itiveness and tenacity. Getting bogged down and having tunnel vision when a challenge arises is not the way to handle them. Instead, accept the challenge, address it and chart a path forward (as quickly as possible). You can do it! Just remember, there *is* a solution. Recognize it, fix it, and keep going!

If you tend to worry about the what-ifs in life, this might be the wrong business for you. If you anticipate the what-ifs, and are able to make decisive decisions, you're more likely to be successful in this business. Things happen all the time. It's part of life. Roll with the punches and keep on swinging!

"NEVER LET THE FEAR OF STRIKING OUT GET IN YOUR WAY."
—Babe Ruth

Throwing in the towel at the first challenge or surprise not only thwarts your chances for financial freedom, but it also stunts your personal growth and keeps you from obtaining the skills necessary to handle the really tough stuff.

Following a tried and true method for fixing and flipping will help you achieve your goals. Others have gone before you. They've had the same challenges, the same surprises, and they've weathered the storms and have come out on top. You can too!

How quickly can I get started?

Even though you're anxious to get started, take the time to map out your plan of action. Compile a list of each of the following players and plan to call and interview them.

- Real Estate Agent(s)
- Potential Lenders
- Real Estate Attorney
- General Contractor(s)

You'll also want to develop your marketing plan to attract and create fix and flip opportunities. (We'll discuss this in depth later)

With these initial team players on hand and analyzed, and your marketing plan in place and operating, you can be on the path to closing on your first fix up property within 45 to 90 days.

AMAZON.COM STARTED WITH ONE LINE OF CODE.

There is a process for success in this business. It begins with daily steps toward your goal; find it + fix it + flip it = freedom!

After just one chapter, you now have an idea of the type of personal skills favor success in this field. You're aware of the incredible potential for earnings and freedom, and what you need to know to begin today!

Today you're reading *Your First Fix & Flip*, I hope you're so excited by it that by this time tomorrow, you're working on step one!

Conclusion

In conclusion, don't be misled by the fix and flip shows you stream. It's possible for you to make very big profits fixing and flipping residential real estate, but it requires a smart analysis, following a tested plan, enormous determination, and hard work. You'll need to gather together a team of the best professionals you can possibly find and then lead them towards your goal. It won't be easy, and you'll make mistakes, but the knowledge you'll gain in this book will help keep those mistakes to a minimum.

CHAPTER TWO
DEVELOPING YOUR OWN LEADS

In this chapter, I'll teach you everything you need to know about creating a complete marketing system so that you can develop your own leads. This way, you won't have to rely only upon realtor listed properties where you'll be in competition with other potential buyers. The methods I'll teach you in this chapter will keep a steady stream of below market priced properties coming your way. Pick at least a few of these marketing methods and keep them running in the background of your business to assure your success!

The key to success in the fix-and-flip business is the ability buy properties at a discounted price, so there is room to fix them and flip them for a profit! In order to do this, we've got to develop our own leads and not rely only on realtor listed properties, where we have to bid against other potential buyers.

I've developed a better way to find houses that are for sale or could be for sale. Sometimes owners have properties that are rentals, and they're tired of being a landlord, or possibly a property that has become run down or sitting vacant. Maybe a relative has died recently and left a property that needs to be disposed of.

At this point the owner might not have even thought about selling.

How do you go about finding houses that would be great flips? Simply put, you develop your own leads. Don't panic! We'll talk about how.

Marketing is always job #1.

When it comes to the fix and flip business, marketing is always job #1. Without your first property to fix and flip, or "the next" fix and flip property, you have no opportunity to make money. There is nothing more important than to ensure your marketing activities are in place, automated and consistent, to ensure the next deal is always there for you to fix and flip, or just flip.

If you control the inventory—you'll control the fix and flip market in your city and have multiple avenues to accumulate wealth.

It's important, especially as you get started on your first fix and flip to set-up your marketing tasks, so they are automated—you don't have to physically do anything on a daily basis to ensure you're always farming for deals—it's automated.

Just as a farmer plants seeds in the spring to harvest a full crop in the fall—you'll be planting your marketing seeds consistently, to ensure you always have the next deal ready to move on.

"MARKETING IS LIKE SEX: EVERYONE THINKS THEY'RE GOOD AT IT."
—Steve Tobak

Create multiple avenues.

The following is a list of resources and activities I've used in my search for properties to buy, fix, and flip.

Part of my schedule quarterly is to spend time analyzing, adjusting current marketing plans, and developing new activities, which will result in a steady stream of properties to buy, fix and flip.

Now I understand if you're starting a brand-new business you may not have the funds to begin with an elaborate, consistent marketing plan. But there are a few really cheap and effective methods of marketing and the most important one is probably printing up business cards, another is just a simple flyer passed out door to door.

We spoke previously about an elevator pitch to lawyers and bankers—now let's talk about one to the general population. Possibly something like "I just began my home renovation business. I refurbish tired, ugly old homes making them beautiful again" and, if the opportunity arises "do you know any for sale?"

This way at the grocery store, bank, and car wash, you can hand out your business cards. You never know who has a rundown house to sell cheap AND it will get you comfortable talking to strangers about his new venture. When you can smile and tell the waitress about your new business, then you are ready to tell the estate attorney about it.

I've always said, "the harder I work, the luckier I get," so while I acknowledge that certain marketing activities can be expensive at times, if you're consistently telling others about your new business, and handing out your business cards, it is possible that you get very lucky within weeks or a month.

All that being said, you really should have a business entity in place such as a DBA ("doing business as" you can easily search and register a name on-line with your Secretary of State). Additionally, it's really important to have some financing in place already, because if you have a good deal fall in your lap, you'll look a bit silly and unprofessional if you're not ready to go.

So, on to the marketing activities;

1. Postcard mailing—My number one tool for acquiring properties is postcard mailing. Decide on an area of town you're interested in buying a house in and consistently mail a postcard to five hundred to fifteen hundred homes. Postcards can be designed, printed, and mailed fairly inexpensively—I love the service Vistaprint.com.

When I was a realtor mailing postcards, or any consistent marketing, it was called "farming." We found if we continued to plant seeds in the same area over, and over, we'd eventually harvested some great properties.

2. Door Hangers—This is simply a twist on the postcard-mailing tactic and it's even less expensive! A door-to-door hanger once per quarter gets attention that even a mailing may not. You do however have to keep an eye on those you hire to distribute the hangers, to ensure that it's actually being done. If you're not busy in fixing and flipping a home currently, get out and hang these yourself, you'll have an opportunity to run into some homeowners—who knows who you'll meet!

3. Estate Sale Companies—Introduce yourself to key people at estate sale companies, they are worth their weight in gold! Take them to lunch, do a pop-by visit. They tend to be one of the first companies to be aware of situations where someone has died or moved into a nursing facility and the family is trying to decide what to do with the home. Create a win-win situation. Help them offload the property easily, while creating an opportunity for yourself! This is a great, cheap, and effective marketing strategy, be certain to have business cards and give them out as you introduce yourself and collect business cards.

With contacts like these on this list, this isn't a one-time "hello …" Establish on-going lines of communication. What can you do for them? Can you refer them to the person you know that is moving into assisted living?

4. Estate Attorneys—I sent out a mailer to five hundred estate attorneys. On the very first mailing this tactic resulted in a call from an attorney with a client that had a home to sell… her ex-husband had died, and she was left to handle the estate.

5. Bird Dog—Identify the one person you know (we all know at least one) who seems to know everyone, and who always seems to have their finger on the pulse of what's going on. Make sure that person knows you're now in

the fix and flip business. Recruit them to acquire leads for you and reward them for their efforts. They would love to help you!

6. Pastor, Priest, or Rabbi—Don't be a "secret agent," let these individuals, and others, in your extended circles, know you're fixing-up and flipping houses. These people tend to know when someone has recently died, is heading into an old-folks home, and divorcing, and so on. In these types of situations, many sellers prefer a quick cash deal.

7. Facebook Ads—Zip code targeted Facebook ads are great for one very simple reason; nearly everyone in America spends time on Facebook! What creative ad can you put together to attract fix-up / estate properties?

8. Small Classified Ads—In Denver, where I live, there are several small neighborhood-type newspapers; Life on Capitol Hill, Out Front, Washington Park Review, Aurora Centennial, etc. I have a simple classified ad in half dozen newspapers like this—Just one deal pays for these ads for years and years.

"IT'S NOT WHAT WE DO ONCE IN A WHILE THAT SHAPES OUR LIVES, IT'S WHAT WE DO CONSISTENTLY."
—Tony Robbins

Properties not listed.

The goal as a fix and flip developer is to find properties that are not yet listed with a realtor. Once the property is listed with a realtor, you'll be competing with everyone on the planet to buy the home—additionally, if you can buy the property before it's listed, you'll buy it for less than the listed price, just by the mere fact that the seller won't have to pay a commission. Once you've settled in on a few neighborhoods, drive the neighborhoods at least once a month. If you have the opportunity to chat with anyone in the neighborhood, introduce yourself, give them a business card and tell them what you do.

INSIDER SECRET: *If you're competing with other buyers on a home listed with a real estate agent, let the listing agent know you'll let them keep the full commission if your deal gets accepted! On a $300,000.00 property, this is as much as $9,000.00 in additional commission the agent would earn with your deal—you'll know by your analysis if the numbers work for this strategy on the home… let the 9-grand go, you're working towards a big paycheck.*

Hand written notes.

Hand written thank you notes after a conversation are critical. The person that bonds with a potential seller will ultimately be the person that gets to buy the house.

Years ago, when I was an active real estate agent the lifeblood of my business was listing homes, if you controlled the listing inventory, you controlled your time. Often, I was competing with other agents to get the listing on the home. In order to give myself a competitive advantage, after my initial appointment, I'd send ½ dozen red roses thanking them for the opportunity to meet with them, ending with "Remember, when you list your home with Jeff Hammerberg, you'll come out smelling like a rose."

On another occasion there was particularly desirable project I was trying to get a listing appointment with the builder on. I was finally able to book an appointment, and this time, prior to the appointment, I was determined to have my company and my marketing skills stick out! I sent the builder a FedEx package, and inside the package was a single shoe with a note tied to the laces that said "Thank you. Now that I've got my foot in the door, I'm confident that when we meet, you'll see the benefits of my company representing you…"

What are some creative ideas you have to show the seller your interest in not only the home, but also in them, and their situation? We live in an information age and people are overwhelmed by information, so it can be difficult to get their positive attention. We can also live in a somewhat rude society, so "thank you" notes are shocking in a pleasant way.

Post card campaign.

From the results of my postcard mailing campaign in mid-2016, I received call from a gentleman whose father had died a year prior. The family was just now starting to investigate selling a duplex the father and mother owned.

The father was a hoarder, and the property (both units plus the garage) were full to the brim of his collections over the past 50 or so years. The mother was still alive, though she had moved out into a retirement community nearby.

At the time I first visited the property, one side of the duplex was occupied by an alcoholic adult son, and the second unit was occupied by an emotionally unstable daughter.

The call I received was from a brother (one of 9 siblings) that lived out of state.

On my first visit, I met the mom (82 years old) who showed me through one of the units, apologizing for the condition of the property during much of the tour. I reminded her there was no need to apologize. I was here to help the family in any way that I could. After all, this is what we do. We often come in after a death, divorce, financial catastrophe or other traumatic event. It's often difficult for members of the family to get together "on one page" and make the decisions necessary to move-on with life. It's important that we arrive with compassion, patience, and a desire to assist the family through this event.

On this property, from the first visit to negotiating a deal and getting to closing, it took several months, lots of patience, and some concessions that were important to the family;

1. I agreed to buy the property "as-is, where-is" no inspections, conditions or appraisals. I could see the structure was sound, did a complete and through

walk-though, and understood the general disrepair of the property. I understood, as with all fix and flips, there would be a surprise or two.

2. I allowed them to leave anything in the property they did not want to take. (We eventually hauled away five 30 yd. dumpsters of "treasures," trash and debris)

3. I allowed them to continue to use the 4-car garage and sort through the father's belongings for 60 days after closing. Items of value in the home that they wanted to keep, were brought to the already overflowing garage.

4. Additionally, I allowed them to have "yard sales" at the property even after we closed, to help them sell off any of the more valuable items.

… These are just to name a few.

The out-of-state brother and I continued throughout this process to keep the communication lines open. I may have done a hundred of these deals in my lifetime, but for this family (and most) this is a huge event! We spoke at least weekly.

The 82-year-old mom and a couple of her daughters worked tirelessly sorting, organizing, clearing and selling the contents for weeks before closing, as I started walking contractors through to get bids.

INSIDER SECRET: *Don't wait until you own the property to get contractors and subs into the property. Take advantage of every moment between getting the property under contract and closing. Start planning your attack! You should be ready on day one to demo! Time is money!*

Per the family's request, the older alcoholic son was not even made aware of the sale. A week before closing, he stayed with his sister "while a contractor did some work on the property," at which time we closed. We changed locks and got to work.

Of course, we had surprises as we rehabbed the units:

- Mold in both basements (professional mitigation necessary, twice!)
- Main sewer line issues.

  We eventually discovered there was a sink hole in the street at the city connection and our main sewer line was collapsed! Yikes. Just because it's in the street, under a city street doesn't mean the city will take responsibility and repair it. This is a fix and flip, time is of the essence… we repaired it ourselves.

- High levels of radon. (We installed mitigation in both units)

  Additionally, we had to install all new electrical panels, as we updated the interior electrical, adding GFI outlets, hard-wiring smoke alarms, updating and upgrading the kitchen, appliances, etc.

This is part of the fix-and-flip business. You always budget in a contingency and you always watch other costs carefully… even with "super unexpected" surprises, you should be able to get through them on-time and on-budget.

Here is the down and dirty on what we did on this property;

Duplex; each unit 900 s.f. up and 900 s.f. down = 1800 s.f. x two

Purchase price; $550,000.00

Rehab costs, including cost of money, survey and attorney; $200,000.00

Closing costs including real estate commissions; $50,000.00

Unit one with a 3-car garage sold for $485,000.00 (We actually could have held out and sold this unit for more—but again, time is money)

Unit two with a 1 car garage sold for $479,000.00

Total investment; $800,000.00

Total sales price; $964,000.00

Net profit pre-tax; $164,000.00

*On this deal, I borrowed 100% of the purchase price and used 100% of my own money (120k cash and credit cards) for the fix-up costs.

YOUR FIRST FIX & FLIP

So, after taxes I earned about $130,000.00 on my $120,000.00 cash investment. How's that for a return!!

Here was a seller that had gotten bogged down by serious problems that they couldn't solve. Here I am, getting a serious price discount on the asset because I, the investor, can solve the problems that the homeowner can't… make sense?

Finally, this is what I'd say about postcards. Mailing out postcards is a numbers game. If you mail out 1000 postcards you will likely get 1-5 semi-serious leads. I would emphasize that it is a statistical numbers game. Therefore, again, you really should have your financing in place FIRST.

So, let's say that you spend $200-$500 on a big postcard mailing that yields 4 leads and 1 excellent lead that turns into a purchase, fix and flip making you $30,000 in profit. Well, then the money spent makes sense. Maybe put it on a credit card?

Bird dogs.

I mentioned this briefly earlier, as an opportunity for income. In this instance we're working with bird dogs (individuals) that work daily to bring fix-up properties to fix and flip developers.

How do you find a bird dog? They'll typically find you! I've found one or two through my hard money lenders—a deal they may have personally passed on, but because of our relationship, they forwarded to me. And secondly, they find you by calling you from the small classified ads your running in the neighborhood papers.

> "IF YOU TURN THE IMAGINATION LOOSE LIKE A BIRD DOG,
> IT WILL OFTEN RETURN WITH THE BIRD IN ITS MOUTH."
> —William Maxwell

Bird dogs are different than your friends that keep an ear peeled to the ground and let you know of potential opportunities. A real bird dog has developed relationships with estate companies, attorneys and key individuals that are a part of a network that they work daily. Many have been working their neighborhood for years and know everything that is going on.

Bird dogs can be extremely loyal to you once you establish that relationship, unlike wholesalers that bring properties to the masses, your bird dog has the opportunity to notify you of the deal first!

This is a great relationship to nurture.

Mowed or not?

As you drive through the neighborhoods, if you see a run-down house, or a yard that needs mowing, jot down the address and find out who owns the house. You can go to the city or county records typically online and get the name of the owner. Once you have that information find their phone number via Whitepages.com. Call them up and see if they have any interest in selling their home.

Here's my script; *Hello Mr. Jones—My name is Jeff Hammerberg, I'm a real estate investor living and working in your neighborhood. I noticed your property at "street address" and was wondering if you had any interest in selling the home?*

Always make sure to drop a handwritten note thanking them for speaking with you and include your business card and contact information.

Estate attorneys.

Estate attorneys are great sources for leads and referrals. We live in an aging society—baby boomers are placing their parents in residential/senior living, and some are moving themselves. As this happens the family homes are being sold off, and a majority of them have aged with their residents, needing updates and upgrades to command new market values.

Any family dealing with issues related to aging are seeking the advice of an estate attorney. A great estate attorney will present the family they represent with many choices and options for every facet of this next phase of their life—your goal will be to establish yourself as the trusted residential real estate expert.

Whether the property works as a fix and flip opportunity, or you bring in your real estate agent to assist, it can become a win-win-win for everyone involved.

Again, this is not about you, it's about best solutions for your potential client.

This would be my advice on estate attorneys. Potentially, this is a really cheap and effective method of marketing.

I would advise that you first go to your "Secretary of State" website and register your business name, that will make you and your new enterprise look professional. Then, go to Vistaprint.com and print up around 1000 business cards. Carry business cards EVERYWHERE.

Now, go to lawyer search sites like avvo.com and search for estate attorneys in your city. This will pull up the local estate attorneys with the highest profiles. There may be 20-30, perfect.

Get busy in the evenings or over a weekend and send a brief, friendly letter to these estate attorneys introducing yourself and your new home restoration business. Explain that you are a cash buyer and close quickly on estate properties. Be certain to include your business card. Mail and then give it 7-10 days.

Try to call and catch the attorney on the phone or leave a voicemail. Then, follow up once a month or so. Voicemails are fine. Just explain that you're an expert in renovating homes and would love to purchase any estate properties; quick close, no inspections, for cash. You're happy to speak with them or their clients—never an obligation.

To register your DBA name, buy business cards, and send the letters, it might be a hundred dollars.

Real estate agents.

Your real estate agent should become your best friend! A great real estate agent will work tirelessly for you in not only helping to scout out great deals, but in analyzing properties that you find, to determine ARV (After Repair Value).

A good real estate agent or broker can also help you to understand the market, where it is now and where it's headed. They can write and present offers for you. They understand real estate rules, regulations and practices. Prior to making an offer, a realtor may be able to find out more information about the seller's motivation, key factors when it comes time to make an offer.

A reputable real estate agent knows neighborhoods where houses are selling, they can provide you with comparables of the houses that have sold and why they sold for what they did. Often real estate agents are privy to homes that are not on the market, a distinct advantage in the competitive fix and flip business. With access to the Multiple Listing Service or MLS, a realtor has a large pool of homes from which to choose. The disadvantage here is the competition also has access to it.

While having a knowledgeable real estate agent on your team is important, your #1 priority is still to find potential fix-up houses on your own—properties that are not yet listed with a real estate agent.

Having a solid real estate agent behind you, you can still do most of the legwork knowing that you've got great backup and someone with a wealth of experience. Your agent can help with a ten-minute market evaluation on properties you find that will be invaluable to you down the road. A ten-minute evaluation is an automated-value that most agents can provide you.

There is also something you can do on your own. Zillow Zestimates is getting better and better with quick down and dirty "current market values" in many markets. www.zillow.com/find-your-home. It's worth the time to check it out.

With any "automated system" in an industry with millions of variables, it's tough to always get it right. I read a few months ago that Zillow was being sued over Zestimates. Anyone can be sued over anything, so who knows? The problem is their algorithm. People feel they are being screwed in some markets because the Zestimate is lower than what they feel the market price of their house really is. Just FYI. Be careful here. The best estimate will always be provided by your real estate agent partner.

This being said, I'm not sure how "people are being screwed," unless they are naive enough to list their home for sale on Zillow, using their numbers, without an accurate Competitive Market Analysis (CMA) done by a local, licensed, professional real estate agent.

After you do find the perfect fix-up house and it comes time to make an offer, your real estate agent can be instrumental in writing a deal that will be accepted.

Should you need to get out of the deal, the real estate agent is adept at inserting contingency clauses such as "subject to a satisfactory home inspection" (and many others) that can give you an out if something unexpected is discovered. (We'll cover more of that in future chapters.)

Going through the interviewing process with real estate agents, make sure you get along with them. The team you build must be cohesive and congenial, as well as smart.

Don't be afraid to ask questions;

1. Are they working with any other buyers who flip houses?
2. How long have they been a licensed agent?
3. Will they represent you exclusively as a buyer's agent?
4. How motivated are they, and how quickly do they respond to calls, text messages and requests?

5. Are they in the business full-time and available 24/7?

Additionally, your real estate agent should be a real advocate for you and will be the key person to go to when it's time to flip/sell your house. In fact, they may possibly be able to line up potential buyers the closer you get to formally listing the property.

They can help you determine ARV (After Repair Value). Developing and nurturing a relationship with a qualified realtor will fortify your position now and in the future.

A real estate agent is a great source for finding other team members, like contractors and sub-contractors, designers, landscaping people, roofers, etc. with great reputations, working in the residential industry.

Wholesalers.

It's typically pretty easy to find wholesale companies, they're advertising on spots like Craigslist touting their properties and services, and you can easily contact them there. Once again, like bird dogs, they'll most likely find you.

Its tough buying properties through wholesalers. Again, the properties are being advertised to the masses. You'll compete with every fix and flip developer in the area. There are some deals, but if you were a wholesale company and had a property listed that received 30 bids, whose bid would you accept?
- The highest price?
- The quickest close?
- The person you've closed a deal with before?
- Or a combination of the three?

It's always about relationships—so build those.

Many of the properties listed with wholesale companies have pretty thin margins. So, if you're a fix and flip developer running multiple jobs, with multiple crews, and you're in and out quick, you have an advantage over a one man show. You can work on those projects that offer less profit, it's only 1 of the 10 jobs you're currently renovating!

With wholesale deals, you're always required to visit the property during pre-scheduled showing slots. Once you're registered with a wholesale company and you've viewed the listing, you can typically place a bid on-line.

HUD / foreclosures.

I've been in the real estate business long enough to know that everyone (regular home buyers and fix and flip buyers) is looking for a foreclosure opportunity, everyone. But in my 27 years of residential experience, I've sold ONE (1) HUD home and no foreclosures.

Granted; #1 it really was never my focus and #2, it's a little more difficult to find and secure HUD and foreclosure deals in a constantly rising market, like mine was, vs. in a city that may have a very depressed housing market.

In about 1998 there was a group of 4 to 5 properties that were being foreclosed on by the City and County of Denver. This is back in the day when foreclosure auctions were held on the courthouse steps. The properties were being auctioned off one at a time, with the total expected to be in the neighborhood of a million or million and a half dollars, oh, and you had to have cash (certified funds) at the auction.

My hard money lender, the guy I still work with today brought the deal to my attention, and collectively we spent the morning of the auction going from bank to bank (his banks, not mine) getting $250,000.00 here and $500,000.00 there, another $100,000.00 over here and $50,000.00 there, until we had about 1.5 million in cashier's checks.

It was an amazing beautiful sunny day in Denver and there were about 50 people lining the steps of the courthouse. Time after time, house after house, we bid and outbid everyone there and bought every property—we were rock stars! I know people thought, "Who are these guys?" Well, the story doesn't end there. With these type of auctions, at least this particular auction, the homeowner had the opportunity to redeem their properties. They had x number of days to pay the outstanding debt, plus penalties and any interest that had accumulated, including the interest on our money... and they did.

All that plotting, and the analyzing, all that running around, all that money being tied up, and we gained nothing except a good story.

As for HUD homes, they are typically offered only to homeowners, people that will buy the home and live in it as their personal residence. The properties are opened up for bidding to investors (you and I) only after a period where it has not sold to potential homeowners.

Tax sales.

As for tax lien properties, I've not personally purchased any houses via this avenue, or attended any tax sales. My hard money lender and I were recently speaking about them, and he believes there is a current opportunity.

In a tax deed sale, a property with unpaid taxes is sold at auction. The sale is used by states to collect unpaid property taxes and differs state-to-state.

Generally, as an investor you'd step in and bid, with and against other investors, on paying off the unpaid taxes. The homeowner has a period of time "redemption period" to pay the outstanding taxes (those that you have now paid).

If the homeowner pays back the taxes during this period, you get paid interest in your money, and a return of your money = bust, waste of time. If the redemption period passes and the homeowner has not paid back the taxes, you have the right to foreclose—which of course has a whole new set of rules and regulations, not to mention the expense.

If you'd like to deal with tax sales, please do your homework and understand the business you're getting into. That's another book or seminar.

Conclusion

In conclusion, you may not have realized from the fix and flip television shows what a huge role marketing plays in finding a low priced, diamond in the rough property that is perfect to refurbish and flip. There's always a steady supply of these properties available in the marketplace, but they don't just fall into your lap. Consider your personality and then choose a few of the marketing methods I've discussed. Keep them running in the background of your business at all times. It's crucial to your success as a residential flipper that you always have a steady stream of potential flip properties coming to you. A real estate flipper with no properties to flip is stalled or out of business.

CHAPTER THREE

FINDING THE RIGHT PROPERTY

In this chapter, I'll teach you how to choose the perfect property for your first residential fix and flip! You should be prepared to look at many properties. If you are lucky, you may find a cheap house needing only cosmetic repairs. That alone could net you a quick $10,000 to fund future ventures. No doubt you'll see some houses that really should be torn down. I'm here to teach you how to evaluate which houses you should fix and flip for a profit, and which houses you should avoid. Let's get started!

With your team of experts assembled, and your target neighborhood determined, it's time to go out and find the right house for you to fix and flip! Don't be impatient. It can take a while to find the right property.

Even though you're anxious to get started, take the time to do your research and find the house that can be turned into a profitable flip. Take a deep breath and know the right house is out there.

Several things need to be evaluated by you, the fix and flip developer, when finding and flipping a house. From locating the right house to fix, to analyzing the neighborhood, to looking at current market trends and weighing the risks. You've got some homework to do.

At first, it may all sound daunting, but with practice and discipline, this part of fixing and flipping will be fascinating and fun and will help establish your business on solid ground.

When evaluating properties, there are certain items of which you need to be aware right off the bat: Many homes built before 1980 contain asbestos in old floor tiles, ceiling tiles, roof shingles and flashing, siding, insulation, (around boilers, ducts, pipes, sheeting, fireplaces) pipe cement, and joint compound used on seams between pieces of sheetrock. Some newer houses may also contain asbestos.

Lead paint is another consideration. It is the most significant source of lead exposure in the United States. Most homes built before 1960 have heavily leaded paint. In fact, some homes built as late as 1978 may also contain lead paint. Depending on city, county, state and national rules and regulations, you may have to professionally mitigate the old paint, or at the very least test, and cover—this can become quite expensive.

The age of the wiring must also be considered. In North American in construction between the 1960's and mid 1970's, aluminum wiring was used to wire whole houses. This was due to the high price of copper at the time. If the home does have aluminum wiring, it is important that the wiring be pigtailed at each outlet—there may be other requirements depending on your jurisdiction.

These things shouldn't stop you from buying a specific property, but they are things to keep in mind.

While you're out looking, be sure to take quality photos of the houses you like, the ones best suited for fixing and flipping. When you look at a lot of houses, details can escape your memory. Having a photo and notes about each house that interests you will help you to make your decision and eliminate confusion about which house had this or that.

Remember not all available properties have sales signs in the front yard. Check out newspapers and neighborhood ads in your search. You can go online as well and check for houses on Zillow.com, Craigslist.org and dozens of other sites. Just remember, that's what your competition will also doing. With any of these sites be careful to ensure the property is real and actively for sale. When in doubt, check with your real estate agent. When viewing properties, keep in mind, some houses might need many more repairs than you think, or are able to see.

Potential money pits.

Some of you may remember the 1980's move "The Money Pit" with Tom Hanks and Shelly Long. Don't let it become your story, the story of a beautiful house, gorgeous, an old gem, but you just keep uncovering more and more problems, and eventually you cry and go broke. Money pits are synonymous with "tear downs."

You don't want to get into a money pit, especially on your first flip. Some houses can't be saved. It's important to know which ones need TLC, added curb appeal, and an overhaul, and which ones need to be torn down. A contractor can help you to determine the difference on your first few homes.

Be wary of drug houses, especially meth houses. I won't touch them. Meth houses are still around and if you wind up looking at a house with plastic covering all the walls, that's likely been a meth house.

In Colorado since the legalization of marijuana we're seeing "grow houses" that have either been abandoned, or have been busted, and now sit vacant and contaminated. Inadequate ventilation in these homes can cause a number of problems. When the humidity gets so high (no pun intended) from the marijuana grow, mold will grow and become severe, eventually causing rot, which will begin to digest the building materials. And we haven't even touched on State disclosure laws when it comes time to sell the house.

If the house has serious foundation issues, you might want to pass—I personally won't deal with foundation issues. There are too many unknown questions in repairing and will it last + will your buyer be satisfied. If it's a failing porch that I can tear off and rebuild, that's one thing, but structural issues with the homes foundation are another.

Check out the plumbing and sewer system, make sure there are no hidden surprises. Is everything running and flushing as it should? Any water marks on the basement walls showing previous issues? I'd recommend always having a sewer scope done, your replacement buyer will!

If the bones of the house are good, often the worst looking house in the neighborhood is an excellent choice to buy. Be sure to check out the property, the lay of the land. If the house is on a hillside, how stable is it? Is the house in a flood zone?

You may get only one shot at touring your prospective house. Make the tour work for you. Look beyond the surface and do some investigating on your own. This will pay off in the long run.

Check for leaks or signs of water damage throughout the house. Look under sinks, around toilets, check the ceilings. If you find damage, determine what caused the problem. Does the house need a new roof, foundation repairs or major electrical system updates?

o   Does the house have insulation?
o   How old is the furnace, roof, windows, electrical, plumbing and air conditioner?
o   Do all the rooms have heat and A/C vents?
o   Is there any sign of mold or mildew?
o   Are there odd odors in the house or sewer gas?

Your answers will help determine your rehab costs. Jot down your findings on a property evaluation form, available at www.FixAndFlip.com. If you're unsure of your ability on your first flip, have your contractor walk through with you to analyze and point out any trouble spots, the negatives and positives of the property.

Cosmetic, minor or major rehab.

Is the house you're looking at in need of only cosmetic repairs? Does it just need some TLC, paint and sprucing up? Cosmetic flips are a little rarer today than they once were. They tend to get snapped up quite quickly.

COSMETIC.
With a cosmetic rehab you're generally looking at paint and carpet. You should be able to be in and out within a couple of weeks. Cosmetic rehabs require the least amount of work, and typically provide the smallest amount of profit.

MINOR.
With a minor rehab you're looking at paint, carpet, replacing some lighting fixtures and possible a reface in the kitchen and baths. With a minor rehab you should be looking at 30 days to finish and be back on the market.

MAJOR REHAB.
With a major rehab, which is typically what you'll be looking at, you'll pretty much be touching everything between the roof and foundation. Not everything will need to be gutted and replaced. You may have perfectly great textured walls that only need to be cleaned of smoke residue and repainted, but you also may be removing and replacing walls, upgrading the HVAC systems, replacing electrical panels and re-plumbing / rewiring large portions of the home.

A major rehab allows you the greatest opportunity for profit. You should be buying this type of property well below market and selling it for a handsome profit.

Buy low—flip quick!

Now here's a thought—if you buy a property at such a bargain that you can make a quick $10,000.00, $20,000.00 or more on a quick flip, doing nothing, should you take the money and move on?

There will be opportunities. You've already analyzed the numbers and you know where you stand in the deal, so what is that walk away number? Remember with either bottom line number you'll have taxes to pay, so add that number into your calculations.

Other considerations;
- Do you have the time and crews for this job?
- Is there another property vs. this available to start?
- Is it worth the time and effort?

An additional consideration will be the legality of a quick purchase a flip. When you bought the property, did you disclose that you may have the opportunity to flip the home for a profit, without doing a thing? Were you required to disclose this, and did you? Ask a real estate attorney about state laws. An agent or broker might be required to disclose but an investor who is not licensed probably has no duty to disclose.

Licensed real estate agents are required to disclose certain activities in a transaction, which is a good thing—it helps to protect homeowners from unscrupulous lenders, contractors and the like.

Choosing a neighborhood. (Coffee house quotient)

When you find a likely candidate for flipping, take the time to check out the neighborhood. Find out what the neighborhood is really like;

1. How quiet is the neighborhood?
2. Do neighbors keep up their properties?
3. Are quality schools close to the house?
4. Any problems or crime in the neighborhood?
5. How many homes are for sale, and are they selling quickly?
6. Proximity to jobs and mass transit?

A few good questions asked early on can be helpful in making the right decision. You might want to determine if the homes in the area are owner occupied or rentals.

UP AND COMING NEIGHBORHOODS.
Many fix-and-flip contractors are hesitant to go into "up and coming" neighborhoods. Yet, with the current market in Denver, people are fighting to buy into these neighborhoods. Five years ago, many of these neighborhoods were considered undesirable, not crime ridden, more industrial / edgy. Yet today some of these exact neighborhoods are commanding the highest prices.

BUZZWORTHY NEIGHBORHOODS.
Buzzworthy neighborhoods have a neighborhood coffee shop. It's a good indication that the neighborhood is "up and coming," if it's not already there! If there is a coffee shop in the neighborhood, it's worth considering.

INSIDER SECRET: *There are typically more opportunities to find the right fix and flip opportunities in fringe or questionable neighborhoods. The coffee shop quotient does work. It doesn't have to be a Starbucks to show the neighborhood is up and coming.*

First time flippers might find themselves with a quandary. For instance, you find a house that needs work and the numbers look great, you believe you can purchase the house at a reasonable price, but it's in a neighborhood you might not feel comfortable living in or working in.

Let's look at some issues that can arise with houses in what can be considered marginal neighborhoods;

- What do the sold comparables tell you about values?
- How long are houses taking to sell?
- What is the condition of neighboring properties?
- What schools are serving the neighborhood?
- What do the crime statistics say about the neighborhood?

All of these items should be taken into consideration when purchasing any property.

Another consideration—homes several miles away from you or even in neighboring cities might have ticked all the boxes of your perfect fix and flip but think about the amount of time you'll spend driving to and from your project. Distance can become an issue, as the project moves forward. Time is money and spending hours commuting back and forth to your project every day may not make sense. If you're single and flexible, how about just moving in for a few months. It takes what it takes to be successful!

Try finding houses within a specific distance from where you live, whatever works for you. If you can envision yourself driving there every day, then keep the house on the list.

MARKET AGE.

Keep your eye on properties that have market age (have been on the market for a long time). You'll typically find with these homes that there is some functional obsolescence; the kitchen is the size of a closet, or possibly there is no room in the 3rd bedroom for a bed, maybe you enter the home through a bedroom… believe me, I've seen it!

We should be licking our chops with the discovery of any of these types of properties—this is what we do, we re-imagine, we-re-develop, and we re-sell for a handsome profit.

Plus, with market age comes a desperate seller, which equals a potentially great purchase price for us. Someone else's nightmare becomes our dream.

Single family—condominium or income property.

Your first fix and flip project will most likely be a single-family home. It's the majority of real estate in most cities and will likely provide the best return for your time and investment.

Single family homes provide the safest investment and are the most sought-after type of property for individuals and families looking to purchase.

Condominiums that are priced right, and in solid HOA's (Home Owners Associations) offer a great opportunity for quick lipstick fix and flips. In a majority of these you're not worrying about the roof, foundation or major systems as they're covered by the HOA. Watch out for special assessments. The HOA suddenly decides that the condos need a new roof or whatever. The money isn't in the budget, so they decide that every owner now owes them something insane like $10,000 or more. So, look at the budget and see if they are socking away money for capital repairs, big things like roofs, parking lot resurfacing, etc.

When I talk about a "Solid HOA," I'm speaking of a project that is;
* Primarily occupied by owners, not renters.
* Has a sound budget and the required cash in reserves.
* A project that is well kept and managed.
* Has a history of solid sales.

When it comes to income properties I get really excited, but I don't want you to start your first fix and flip with an income property, unless it's a duplex with a relatively minor rehab.

Try to start with something less complicated and straightforward, a single-family home or condominium.

With income property rehabs and conversions (converting from rentals to "For Sale" units) you'll have legal loopholes to jump through, plus you'll have to ensure your city and county allows conversions; from a rental, or commercial, or industrial, to residential "for sale" units.

We'll not discuss the specifics on rezoning that would be required to change the use of a property. Our focus should be on current residential rentals, for conversion to for sale units. The thing I love about conversions, is you're working with the same crew (maybe larger), on one project, in one location, on multiple mostly identical units.

Don't let the age of a house bother you, an older home isn't a terrible thing. I don't have an age criterion. Of my flips, 90% have been in the urban core of Denver, within a 10-mile radius of downtown. So, there have been some as old as the late 1800's.

Speaking of my Colorado Flips, one historic mansion I flipped is now the Nation's First "Bud and Breakfast," The Adagio Bed and Breakfast in Denver, CO.

Is the money there or not?

After you find a candidate for your first flip, now is the time to evaluate whether the money is there. The BMV (Beginning Market Value) for our purposes, is the price at which you bought (or will buy) the property, in its current "before remodeled" state. It's critical to know this number as it's the basis for all calculations and estimates moving forward.

> **BMV + (Fix-up Costs / Cost of Money / Selling Costs) – ARV = Profit before taxes.** Your goal is to get the house at the lowest possible price, to maximum your profit.

The ARV (After Repair Value), the value of your home after it has been re-habbed, is important in determining your profit potential. Armed with this information, you'll know the price at which you can list your flip. That will determine your approximate profit margin and whether to move forward.

The relationship you've established with your real estate agent/broker will be critical in nailing down the REAL / realistic selling price for your completed rehab.

If the initial numbers look good, work with your contractor to hammer out estimated rehab costs and determine the kind of upgrades you want in the home. Again, don't place top of the line appliances in a home where the neighborhood norms don't support them. Make the upgrades suitable for the neighborhood. Knowing your purchase price, fix-up costs, cost of money and selling costs, you can put together a solid offer.

If the home is listed, your real estate agent can determine how long the house has been on the market and can check to see if any offers have been made. This will give you a good idea of where the sellers are in their thought process. You may be able to determine how anxious they are to sell. If they have refused offers in the past, you might be able to determine the reasons and be able to remove those obstacles in your own offer.

With a close look at every detail, you will soon discover that with proper evaluation, risk is mitigated, and profit assured.

10-minute market analysis.

Ask your real estate agent about an "automated value" which is available in most MLS (Metro Listing Systems) nationwide (this is the system only licensed real estate agents have access to). What you're looking for is the value for a "like new—totally remodeled home" in the neighborhood of your flip. Which is what you'll be selling, a "like new—totally remodeled home" at the completion of your remodel.

The automated value process only takes your agent about ten minutes, and you'll have a highly accurate figure for standard homes in the area. With this information alone, you can determine if there is enough profit in a potential listing.

You can also use Zillow Zestimates and your country real estate appraised values as a secondary check, although these will be less accurate.

Thorough real estate agent analysis.

Outside of the automated value process, you'll be looking to your real estate agent for a thorough analysis of the property, not just the quick mathematical process. The quick process is to determine if you should dig deeper or move on to the next potential.

> *"I CAN SHOW YOU WHERE TO DIG, AND WHAT TO DIG FOR, BUT THE DIGGING YOU WILL HAVE TO DO FOR YOURSELF."*
> —Matisyahu

Your real estate agent understands that location matters, condition matters, age and layout matter, upgrades and functionality matter. All of these things will have to be measured against your end product to help determine value. The other things that can help or hurt you will be;

- Location, location, location, in reference to schools, busy roads, etc.
- Available inventory / competition.
- Current mortgage rates and availability.
- Curb / street and neighborhood appeal.
- Physical layout and upgrades.

A through market analysis will cover these areas, in addition to outlining the agents marketing plan, and estimating the time it will take for your home to sell.

Conclusion

In conclusion, once you really get started seeking out below market priced homes to fix and flip for a profit, you are likely to feel a bit overwhelmed with choices, but that's okay. That's what I'm here for. You are looking for that true "diamond in the rough." Your first fix and flip should need updating. Perhaps it was last updated in the 1970's or the 1980's. It should be located in a good school system close to major employers and it should be structurally sound. Lastly, it should be acquired for an excellent price. If you are patient and persistent, you will find your perfect, first residential flip property.

CHAPTER FOUR

NEGOTIATING WITH THE HOMEOWNER

In this chapter, I'll teach you how to connect with the owner of the home you'd like to refurbish and flip. It's important to be professional, honest, and kind towards the homeowner at all times. Your reputation and future business prospects depend upon your excellent behavior. The homeowner may need to sell because the love of his life just passed on or perhaps he needs to enter a nursing home. Your goal is always a win/win situation for both you and the homeowner. Let's get to it!

Building rapport.

Our goal, as we have mentioned previously, is to purchase properties directly from the owner(s). Dealing with an owner directly is much different than negotiating with your real estate agent on a property that is listed by another real estate agent— these are professional negotiations and happen in the life of real estate agents daily.

For a homeowner, being contacted out of the blue by someone wishing to purchase a property, there may be hesitation and suspicion leading the conversation.

The basis of all human relationships and a successful purchase for us, as fix and flip developers, is building rapport with the potential seller. Sellers don't care how much we know, until we show how much we care.

In the initial phone call discover what are the sellers' current needs? What best serves them with moving forward to potentially sell the property? Many times they may be confused about the best path forward, with your expertise you can ask the questions, which may reveal a clear path forward for them.

> *"ONE OF THE BEST WAYS TO PERSUADE OTHERS*
> *IS TO LISTEN TO THEM."*
> —Dean Rusk

Additionally, no matter their current needs, are you able to help them?
- Can you align them with an estate sale company?
- Would they like to speak with a real estate agent?
- Do they need to speak with a real estate attorney?
- Are they looking to move into senior living?
- Would a 1031 Exchange best serve their needs?

With any of these needs you should be able to pull the appropriate person/company out of your database and assist in their investigation and discovery. Who knows this may ultimately end up back in your lap to purchase—after all, you've been the person helping them along all this time.

Occasionally, especially with estate situations you can offer to buy the home with everything in it. "Don't worry about emptying out the house, I'm happy to handle everything for you after closing." I've done this many times and it's a great relief to the homeowner.

Many times, in estate situations you may be dealing with a relative from out of town—they have no idea where to start. For others, this is a traumatic time… they may be headed to the final phase of their life.

Be respectful and open and you'll find that people will be more open to you and your ideas. Find the common ground between you and the road to buying the house that is a benefit to the seller.

Kindness and patience are important virtues to have when dealing with the homeowner or executor. You may have to work with a potential homeowner for a year or longer while they come to terms with where they are, and what they must do.

Sometimes, the toughest wall to tear down is the wall of obstacles erected by a seller. To the seller, it may seem impenetrable, but to you as the buyer, it's an opportunity to help the seller realize that the obstacles can be handled, one by one. Make the process easier for the seller and the wall of obstacles will crumble.

Walk-through analysis.

At some point after all the initial telephone and possibly e-mail conversations with a potential seller (remember, some of the conversations can go on for months), our goal is to get an appointment set to visit the property. Nothing can happen without you getting real face time with the seller, and hopefully that's during a walkthrough of the property you're wishing to purchase.

It's during this initial visit of the property where you'll have an opportunity to ask additional questions about the seller's needs.

After introducing yourself and thanking them for meeting you, let them show you around and tell you about the property and their situation, you'll probably learn everything you'll need to know to best determine your strategy for purchasing.

At the very least when you've finished your walkthrough, you should have the answers to these basic questions;

- Why are they thinking about selling the home?
- When are they thinking about selling?
- What do they think the home is worth?

- What's the most important thing to them in selling the home?

During your walkthrough the seller may recognize the repairs the property needs, or they may believe the property is in excellent shape for its age—again, in either case, this is the time for you to primarily listen and take notes.

It's not our job at this point to point out every flaw with the property or start to beat them up about price or condition.

After your walkthrough, thank them for the opportunity and let them know you'll get back with them (at a specific date and time) after your analysis—set a follow-up appointment before leaving.

Setting the stage.

On your follow-up meeting with the seller it's important to again thank them for the opportunity—it's during this meeting that we'll start to layout where we're at in terms of price, based upon the property condition / market conditions / timing, etc.

INSIDER SECRET: *Listed below are some of the talking points we use when speaking with a seller after we have disclosed price and shown them what kind of investment we'll have to put into the property, without showing them our entire hand.*

- No realtor commissions.
  Real estate commission can be as high as 7%, with us you pay nothing.
- No property inspection.
  You can talk about property inspections and the surprises they may bring; roofs, foundation issues, lead and asbestos—could equal thousands.
- No appraisal.

We have no control over what the lenders appraiser will determine the value to be. One thing is certain, if the appraisal comes in low, you'll have to lower the price.

- We buy the home "as-is, where-is," no clean-out or fix-up of anything by the seller is required.

  What convenience—not a thing to do.

- We'll close exactly when you want, at your convenience.

Items to think about if you listed the home with a real estate agent vs. our buyout offer;

- You provide house clean-out and fix-up.
- You sign a long-term listing agreement with no guaranteed sale.
- You pay a large real estate commission.
- Potential buyers may write offers significantly less than asking price.
- The buyers will do a formal "property inspection" and can ask for thousands of dollars to repair items. *If you don't come to an agreement, they can walk away from the deal and you start over.*
- The property will have to appraise! Will it? *With FHA buyers, no peeling paint, no rotted trim, no leaking gutters, etc., etc.*
- Potential buyers will have to go through loan approval process. *Anything can happen, no guarantee of approval and no knowing until days before closing… weeks after you accepted the contract.*

Negotiation 101.

With all negotiations the goal is a win-win, so that both parties feel good about the end result. The Internet is loaded with articles, webinars and books on negotiating; it's probably one of the most valuable tools you could add to your person toolbox, so add a negotiating class to your goals for this year.

*"IN BUSINESS AS IN LIFE, YOU DON'T GET WHAT YOU DESERVE,
YOU GET WHAT YOU NEGOTIATE."*
—Chester L. Karrass

In negotiating, these are basic rules to follow;

1. Know the person you're negotiating with.
   What are the main motivating factors for them?
2. Have something to offer—don't make your best offer first.
   How can you sweeten the deal when you hit a sticking point? This isn't always cash, it could be timing, financing, as-is, etc.
3. Know when to stop talking.
   At some point, the next person to talk loses. Don't oversell, I see it all the time—you could have shut-up and closed the deal long ago. After an agreement, stop selling!
4. Be kind—play nice.
5. Know the benefits/strengths of your offer.

Removing seller obstacles.

Put yourself in the seller's shoes. Typically, you want to close the deal as soon as possible, say within thirty days. The more you can accommodate the seller's wishes, the better position you'll be in. They might even choose your offer over a higher offer because you agree to close within their timeframe—that could be a quick close, or a delayed close, allowing them time to find other living arrangements, not feel rushed, etc.

Meeting that closing date isn't that big of a deal if you have everything lined up on your end. You can feel confident about giving the seller what they need, and you'll be on your way to fixing your flip.

In real estate, everything is negotiable. Sellers are concerned about how much they'll have to pay from the proceeds from the sale, and you'll want to make sure that you don't pay more than your calculations indicate.

So, who pays and for what? Sellers and buyers have different closing costs. Seller closing costs can include; legal fees, half the closing fees, title insurance, utility escrows and of course, the real estate agent commission.

The buyer's closing costs include; half of the closing fees, mortgage and title insurance, appraisal fees and any loan discount points (if you're getting a loan), escrow fees, etc. Depending on when the house is sold, taxes will be prorated. While the seller's fees are deducted from the proceeds of the sale, the buyer's closing costs are in *addition* to the down payment.

Some states mandate real estate closing costs. Be sure to check if those mandates are in place where you live. In many states, real estate attorneys are involved in every closing. However, in Colorado where I live, only real estate agents and title companies are involved. No attorney is necessary.

Closing costs can be negotiated. If the seller is anxious to be done with the process and is truly motivated, they might offer to pay all closing costs. See what you can do in your offer.

Every transaction you'll be working on will either have a real estate broker involved writing the purchase contract, or if you're allowed legally, and are experienced enough, you can write the offer (which I never really recommend) or hire an attorney.

Writing the offer.

Buying real estate can be a competitive sport, especially in hot markets. It's easy to get caught up in the emotions of the offer process, but as a fix and flip developer, keep emotions out of the game. You want to make the best offer possible based upon your through analysis, which will determine your highest and best offer.

Sure, you're excited about your first flip and the potential it offers. However, it's not a good idea to get overly attached to an individual house—this is a business decision.

Yes, you've done your homework. A lot a time has gone into your due diligence and you're feeling confident that you've found the right flip. You know what you can do with the house, and you have a promising idea of your potential profit.

Yet, things don't always work out. By keeping your perspective and not allowing your emotions to influence your decision, you'll be better able to negotiate the right deal, at the right price.

Other things also come into play with your purchase decision. Market conditions always factor into the deal. While you're out looking for the right house, keep your eye on the market to see what's happening.

Sellers always want the most they can get for their house. Buyers naturally don't want to pay too much. Know what the market supports and implement that information into your offer strategy. What is your agent telling you about current market conditions?

For instance, if the market is trending down because of high inventory or a dip in the economy, adjust your purchase offer accordingly. You must always be looking ahead, you'll be putting this property back on the market after your renovations. If the market doesn't look like it will work in your favor, find a different house and/or wait to see what the market does.

Good market or bad—there will always be deals to be had, and money to be made.

Unlike some schools of thought, I don't like writing ridiculously low offers on multiple properties, I think it's a bad practice, wasting a lot of people's time and energy. Owners can be insulted and will most likely refuse to even consider your deal, finding it laughable or worse, insulting. Guard your reputation, it will follow you all over town and all the days of your life—don't be known as "that guy." Remember, the seller's emotional quotient must figure into this as well, it's not just your emotions involved.

Offering a fair price that gives you and the seller room to negotiate, will work far better than offending the seller. It keeps the dialogue going. Until there is a refusal, you still have a chance to get the house.

Sometimes, we can get upset by a counter-proposal to what we considered a fair offer. Keep cool and keep your emotions out of it. Employ strategy and always be empathetic to the seller. You might have to give a little, but they will also have to do the same thing. Low-ball offers right out of the gate, slam doors on any potential deal.

> **INSIDER SECRET:** *If you can't come to terms that will assure you a decent profit, it's simply not the right deal. Move on. I've lost many deals I was sick about, but there has always been a <u>better deal, better property, more profit</u> waiting for me… get over it and say NEXT!*

In making an offer in slower markets, where houses are taking some time to sell, allowing room for some negotiation is standard.

In a hot market, you're off to the races and often don't have time to dally and negotiate. Do your homework and be ready to act quickly, but not impetuously. Cash is king. Being able to think and move fast are essential.

Hot markets move at an incredible clip, with many houses barely even getting the For-Sale sign in the yard. Expect to pay the asking price or more for homes that are already listed with a realtor in hot markets—in our market here in Denver, CO and many across the country it's not uncommon to have multiple offers the same day a property hits the market.

This is the ideal time to try and alleviate some of the seller's concerns about inspections, appraisals, loan conditions, clean-up, etc. Step up, be creative and make your offer as agreeable and tempting as possible.

After all the research, the hunt for the right house, the right loan, it's time to construct the right offer, one that works not only for the seller, but most important-ly, for you. The offer process can be filled with anxiety, but if you come to the table prepared, and are being represented by an experienced real estate professional, there is no need for worry—trust the process, trust the investigations you've done, and trust the numbers you've run. Now is the time to talk with your agent and put together the strategy and the offer.

There are pertinent points that you should remember in making your offer. Here are some suggestions for writing that winning offer.

1. Professionally prepared offer.

   Sloppy offers show sloppy business practices—the offer should be professionally prepared, legible and on a state approved contract. (Hopefully your agent or attorney is preparing the offer).

   The exception to a full written offer would be providing an "Intent to Purchase" letter, which would just be a one-page document outlining the details and specifics of what you are proposing.

2. Attach a pre-approval letter or verification of funds (bank letter) to the offer, specific to this contract.

   An offer or letter of intent without proof in your ability to close should be quickly discarded by any seller. Make this easy for them. Show them you're ready, willing and able.

3. Earnest Money—Real offers include real money.

   A check should be attached to any offer. Of course, in many cases if you're working with a property owner directly (on a property that is not listed with a realtor), you'll make this check payable to the title company you and your real estate agent work with.

4. A clean offer.

   The ability to waive as many contingencies as possible; Physical Inspection—Loan Approval—Survey, Insurance, Appraisal, etc. This may be the advantage of the seller working with you / accepting your offer vs. the seller listing the home with a realtor and opening the property to an offer from anyone. You're again showing you're serious about the property and won't be back in a week or two or three to beat the seller up for more money on inspection items, etc.

5. The ability to be flexible with the seller on a closing date.
   What if the seller is concerned about their or his/her tenant(s) finding a replacement home or needs additional time to clear out his mother's belongings, or a divorce with some unknown dates. Be compassionate and flexible in extending your closing date if the seller needs it, within reason.

6. The ability to take the property "as-is, where-is"
   Allowing the seller to pack (or not) and leave. "Don't worry about cleaning up the property. Don't worry about the old tires in the back yard. Don't worry about that leaky sink, etc." What a relief to the seller to know he/she only must worry about getting out and moving on to the next phase of his/her life.

7. Finally, what else do you need to feel comfortable signing this offer today?
   Since there are at least two sides to any deal, the seller will have some things on their minds about what they want and what they expect from the deal. It's good to know what those things are in advance, so you can anticipate making an offer that will alleviate their concerns.

Earnest money.

OK, now that you've gotten the offer written up, it's time to make out your earnest money deposit check. This shows good faith in the deal and will help to assure the sellers that you are a serious buyer. But how much of a deposit do you make? As far as earnest money deposits, it's safe to suggest 1 to 1.5% of the purchase price.

I'd always recommend this check be made out to the listing brokerage (company not agent) and or the title company that will be involved with the closing. This is usually a title company the listing real estate agent chooses. When working directly with a seller, never make out the check directly to the seller or have it held by the seller. Things happen and it's best to have a neutral and experienced third-party handling all funds.

There is virtually no risk in losing your earnest money unless you can't perform on the contract that you have written. Remember, you're going to have less "outs" in the contract, if you waive the formal inspection, loan approval, etc. In a typical contract you could rescind the deal for something as simple as "loan terms you didn't like" or "unsatisfactory inspection," in the buyer's (your) subjective opinion. In other words, just about anything.

Even if you waive some of these inspection dates and deadlines, you would still have a few possible outs like a formal appraisal, insurance objection and/or another contingency you want to put in place. Contingencies can be helpful tools in the negotiating process, but too many of them in the offer will overburden it. The offer will not be as strong as it could be. Typically, a seller will find the offer with fewer contingencies more attractive.

By having a home inspection clause in your offer, it is possible to come back to the table and ask for a reduced price, or credit at closing, to cover a newly discovered discrepancy, and quite possibly lower your costs.

One of my pet peeves is a fix and flip developer writing a full price offer on a home the day it hits the market, getting the offer accepted, and then doing a formal inspection and asking for a ridiculous price reduction. This is a lazy tactic for trying to buy properties—pissing off sellers and making everyone in the business look shady. Bad for you, bad for your reputation, and bad for business.

> *"HONESTY AND INTEGRITY ARE BY FAR THE MOST*
> *IMPORTANT ASSETS OF AN ENTREPRENEUR."*
> —Zig Ziglar

After evaluating the house and calculating your costs, you'll know if the money is there to make this flip work for you. Never resort to tricks or gimmicks in buying or selling properties.

On your first fix and flip purchase or two, you do want to leave yourself outs in the contract, but don't lose the deal by pushing the contingency factor. Sellers get nervous when they see an extensive list of items. It might make *you* feel more secure, but the seller will feel otherwise. On the other hand, by not having contingencies in your offer, you may put yourself at risk and the earnest money could be lost if you decide not to go forward. Having appropriate contingencies in place gives you a fail-safe in the offer process.

For your first few fix and flip projects, the home inspection contingency is probably the most important one you must have in the contract. On one hand, it's very important to write a "clean" offer to the home seller, but on the other hand, it's just as important to have at least one legitimate means of getting out of the contract, if necessary.

As a newcomer to the profession, you have a higher risk of missing an expensive repair that could ruin your budget and your profit. Just a few hundred dollars spent on a high-quality home inspection could save you thousands of dollars in earnest money and tens of thousands of dollars in lost profit.

As a new investor, you might not recognize that a decades old roof leak has been recently painted over. An issue like this could cause an extensive growth of mold and negatively impact the home's structural integrity.

Besides the items mentioned above, you may want to include the right to assign the contract to another party, let's say another fix and flip developer, or your lender. By having that ability to assign the contract, you have more flexibility.

It's a smart idea to put in the offer that you'll be allowed to walk through the house 1 day prior to the actual closing. Sometimes, people change things, or that antique fireplace surround goes missing, or something may have happened in the home since your initial walk-through that would alter the condition. That alteration may hit your fix-up budget. Keeping surprises to a minimum is what the fix and flip business is about.

Every offer will include a time limit on when they must sign the offer, plus dates and deadlines for certain contractual events. It's to everyone's advantage and keeps forward momentum.

If the market is hot, sellers have and use much more latitude, they control the shots. By adding a deadline for signing, you can attempt keep control of the situation. Real estate agents working for the seller won't want to hurry in presenting offers to their clients. It allows them time to spread the word that there is an offer on the table. Human nature takes over and things can get very competitive at that point. Other offers may come flowing in, and can even cause a bidding war, something you should avoid because it can greatly reduce your profit on the flip.

Don't get emotionally involved on these offers! You know your "max" buy offer. Stick to it!

Presenting your offer.

When working with the home seller directly you'll want to sit down with the seller and go over your offer in person. If you don't understand contracts and every detail of your offer, you need to have your agent along to answer any questions.

If you do have your agent present your offer to a seller directly, the agent must disclose their role on the transaction. Are they representing you only? Or are they working as a transaction agent, essentially not representing you or the seller.

Sellers net sheet.

When meeting with the seller to present you offer, ensure you or your real estate agent have prepared a seller's net sheet.

A seller's net sheet will provide the seller an estimate of their net proceeds (the amount of money they'll make after expenses) from the sale. A seller's net sheet outlines expenses like closing fees, lawyer fees (if any), real estate taxes, owner's title insurance policy, payoff of any existing mortgages, repair escrows or any other credits to the buyer, and any other possible expenses.

Conclusion

To conclude, the offer you make to the owner of your first residential fix and flip may be very different from that of a traditional buyer. You can offer significant benefits to the seller which will make the sale of his property enormously convenient and stress free. It's important that you and your agent present a clear and clean written offer to the seller that helps him to understand the benefits of working with you and why they exceed anything an ordinary retail buyer can match. Remember to be clear, kind, and professional at all times and you will secure your first fix and flip!

CHAPTER FIVE

FINANCING DEAL #1

In this chapter, I'll teach you one of the most important and intimidating challenges you'll face in residential real estate flipping—where to find the money to begin. As always, creativity and persistence are paramount. I'll explain how I finance my fix and flips, and I'll give you numerous sources you can explore to finance your first fix and flip. Once you've shown your business plan to a few credible sources of financing, you must put pencil to paper to determine how the cost of borrowing money fits in to your budget. It's not as scary as you might think. Let's get to it!

The name of the game with the fix and flip business, like starting up most any business is money—where am I going to get it, how much do I need and what will it cost me.

There is plenty of money around to finance the purchase of real estate in good markets and bad—it's a core piece of our American economy, the growth and stability of our Nation, and individual wealth.

The very thing you want to finance becomes the security for the loan, unlike trying to finance a new sub sandwich shop, or Internet startup business—fail here, and the lender is secure in knowing their money is safe in the property you've purchased.

> *"90% OF ALL MILLIONAIRES BECOME SO THROUGH*
> *OWNING REAL ESTATE."*
> —Andrew Carnegie

No money down deals.

Let me call it like I see it—there are no "no money down" deals that will allow you to enter this business and make a profit, unless it's your grandma, mom or dad.

It's tiring to see late night TV charlatans hawking real estate programs with the "no money down" hook… really? It's 2018 as I'm writing this book and the real estate market is red-hot in a majority of the country. In most of the recognizable markets there are lines of potential buyers with cash in hand, why would anyone let you buy their home with no money?

There are plenty of legitimate ways to finance the purchase and fix-up of your first fix and flip property, save your time and money by not buying into the "I can do this for nothing" story. Honestly, if there is the occasional no money down property available, it's probably way overpriced, or in such a depressed market or area, that it wouldn't make sense to buy it as a fix and flip—it would be your first failed project, not a great way to get started!

Maybe, possibly, perhaps, when the real estate market turns south again (what goes up must come down, or at least correct at times) you can find a deal or two where the owners just wants out and will let you in with zero down… but, if you get in, and the market is that depressed, can you get out?

INSIDER SECRET: *There is money to be made in the fix and flip business whether the market is strong or weak, but you still have to buy the property under value, based upon the current actual market.*

The only legitimate no money down program on the planet is a VA loan, available to honorably discharged veterans and their spouses to buy a primary residence.

Cost of money—your largest expense.

Make sure in your project budget and calculations that you include your cost of money, it will be one of your largest expenses.

Hard money lenders can charge up to 2% per month or more. They are not all that high, but we're using that for a dramatic example.

> Purchase price: $275,000.00
>
> Down Payment: $27,500.00
>
> Principle balance $247,500.00 x 2% per month
>
> $4,950.00 per month until repaid—on a 6-month project we're talking $29,700.00. There would be a huge mistake in your budget and calculations to not remember this number.

You can finance your real estate deal anyway you'd like—preferably the most economical way, but if you're like me when I stared, I didn't want to wait around for the perfect financing, I didn't want to wait around for the perfect credit score, I didn't want to wait around for a rich friend to help me out. I wanted to get started now, make money on this deal, and continue on to the next—eventually financing my own deals and owning some of the real estate I was fixing!

Now you can make a million excuses,
or make a million dollars—what will it be?

Conventional financing.

Finding the right mortgage broker or banker is essential in building your business for the long haul. You'll want to find the person who can track down the best loans at the best interest rates, which are best suited for flippers.

A "mortgage broker" (vs. a mortgage lender) has an overview of lenders that are easy to work with and are experienced at working with flippers who want to sell their houses quickly after the remodel. If you are still working a J-O-B, on your day off, grab a legal pad, a pen, and a cup of coffee. Search Google with the terms "your city" and "mortgage broker." Then, just start calling. Explain to the mortgage brokers that you get on the phone that you are beginning a home refurbishing business. You intend to find undervalued homes in good neighborhoods and fix them up. You plan to hold them for a few months, and then put them back on the market for a higher price.

Ask the mortgage broker who he knows that might be able to finance your projects. This is a good strategy, but it can take a little bit of patience. You may wind up speaking to a dozen different lenders, but that's fine. You should expect to be referred to all sorts of lending professionals, but that's also okay.

Also, don't forget about your personal bank - you may have a good relationship with your banker. Check with them and see how they can help you to achieve your goals. Remember, you're looking for short-term loans. Be sure to tell your banker or broker that you intend to flip the house and will be buying another house as soon as the first one sells.

Adding the right lender is paramount to your success in flipping houses. Establish a good rapport with your lender. Often people think of their lenders as an adversary. However, it's best to cultivate a healthy relationship with your lender or mortgage broker. It benefits both of you. A solid and amicable partnership with your money source can reap rewards for years to come, for you and your lender!

All of that being said, my personal bank of 20+ years, ANB Bank in Denver, CO, has been zero help in financing my fix and flip purchases, or with the fix and flip project costs in terms of a LOC (line of credit).

I decided since I run close to a million dollars through my business account annually that I'd meet with a loan representative and talk about how we may benefit one another in working together on my fix and flip financing.

Essentially what they offered me (825 credit score) was a LOC (line of credit) that had to be secured by collateral. That collateral could be properties I owned, BUT, I would have to pay for an initial appraisal of $750.00 per property, and the properties would have to be re-appraised every year to keep the LOC open.

The banker admitted, this is what they would offer anyone that came in off the street, it didn't matter that I had been banking with them for 20+ years.

With ANB Bank I was starting easy by only asking for a $100,000.00 LOC. (I had more money than that sitting in my checking account). This is the type of "help" you can expect from your typical banker, and that's in a great market… expect worse if the market is shaky at all.

I decided to let them keep all their money.

Hard money lenders.

I prefer to work with a hard money lender on my projects. I know how long the project will take, I'll be in and out quickly, and I know they'll be at closing with the cash—no excuses. Hard money lenders are typically individuals that specialize in quick cash loans secured by the real estate you're buying, without the hassle and fuss of a traditional lender; no appraisals, no inspections, no objections, no rejections.

The only other option I'd consider is more of a traditional lender that specializes ONLY in fix-and-flip financing, so they know the business, they know your business, and they're here to help you get the deal done. Merchants Mortgage (Merchantsmtg.com) would be an example of that here in Denver, CO. Merchants will lend you 90% of the purchase price and 90% of your fix-up costs at a very competitive interest rate. Plus, they understand the business as this is all they do, and they're great to work with.

Other people's money.

You may have heard it said, the "Secret of the rich: use other people's money," but initially that may be tough advice to follow, especially in a new business for you.

You'll notice with this book I'm really just trying to give you exactly what you need to buy, fix and sell your first fix and flip. I'm not going to bore you by writing 10 pages of crap about each type of 6 or 7 mortgages. I'll tell you what you need to do and who you'll need to see to get your first deal financed successfully.

If you're a rocket scientist with Martin Marietta and need to know every detail about every aspect of financing, please buy and read as many books as you need. The rest of us will be making money! (Nothing against rocket scientists, I've had many as great clients)

If you can use 100% of other people's money that's great! Maybe your father is praying you'll finally find something to do with your life, and he'll hand over as much cash as you'd like to start a business. Maybe your sister or best friend hit the lottery, or maybe you just went scuba diving and found a chest of gold.

For me I had none of those options available—I did it the old-fashioned way. I hustled and worked, and worked, and worked, and scrimped, and saved, and found a hard money lender that believed in me, liked my persistence, and loaned me the rest!

For you, it should be easier; you'll have this blueprint to follow—my lessons learned become your great advantage.

Coming up with 10 to 20%.

The great news is, with most hard money lenders you'll typically only need 10% down of your own money, let's look at some sources where we can find that money;

- Tap your 401k or SEO retirement account.
  Make sure to talk with your accountant about this one.
- Home equity LOC against your principle residence.
  This is quite easy and may even be tax deductible, check with your CPA.
- Get a gift or loan from a family member or friend.
  The IRS allows gifts of up to several thousands of dollars per year, with no tax consequences for the giver or receiver.
- Cash advance on your credit card.
  This is expensive money—but if the deal has the room, the money is instantaneous and easily accessible.
- Refinance a paid off automobile.
  Visit your bank or credit union and ask about financing a paid off vehicle. While you're there, ask about an unsecured line of credit.
- Sell unwanted items.

Financing your fix-up costs.

With the financing in place to purchase your fix and flip property, your next step will be to nail down where the money to actually do the flip/rehab is coming from. Much of this may depend on whether you're doing a minor remodel, or a major gut and remodel.

Here are some sources of financing I've used for the actual remodel work;

- Cash on hand or in the bank.
- Home equity LOC via a credit union on my primary residence. (Credit unions are much more liberal with their lending policies than banks)

- Credit cards.
- The hard money lender themselves; property purchase plus remodel costs.
- Personal loans from friends / family.
- Loan from my realtor. (he's getting the listing + interest on the loan)
- Contractor carries some of the material costs through closing.

All of this being said make sure this is part of what your initial planning includes. It does no one good to have you buy a project that you're going to run out of money on during the flip.

In the Denver, CO market Merchants Mortgage, the lender we've mentioned before, will lend you 90% of the purchase price and 90% of your fix-up costs—almost a no-brainer. Additionally, the 10% down they do require on the loan doesn't necessarily have to be cash, they'll accept equity you may have in another property or properties and are happy to explore other options with you.

It really shows the value of working with individuals and companies that specialize in working with fix and flip developers—they understand the business, they understand the value you're bringing to the community, they understand your needs, and they will do everything possible to work with you.

On one of my very, very early flips (we're talking early 90's) I needed cash to finish the project and I had run out of options… what did I own, where could I get the 6 to $8,000.00 I needed to finish the job? At the time the only thing I owned free and clear that had some value was my 5 Series BMW. I noticed the classified ad of a person that did loans against car titles, set an appointment, showed up with my title and got the cash I needed. I still had my car to drive, finished my project, sold it successfully, paid back the loan and was one step closer to the financial freedom I so desired.

*"NOTHING GREAT WAS EVER ACCOMPLISHED
WITHOUT MAKING SACRIFICES."*
—Unknown

There are hundreds of stories way more dramatic than mine. Take for instance Fred Smith, the founder and CEO of FedEx. He once flew to Las Vegas after being denied a business loan he needed to fund fuel costs. He bet his last $5,000.00 on blackjack to keep his company alive—and won. Without the risk, FedEx would not be here today!

What is your level of commitment to changing the course of your life, to funding your new fix and flip business, to doing everything possible (and even the impossible) to ensure your success.

Use me, fly free.

INSIDER SECRET: *One of the things I love to do, is use my Southwest Airlines credit card (I have a personal and business card) to finance my fix-up materials and supplies. You can imagine, I don't (and most of my family doesn't) pay for travel anywhere that Southwest fly's. I have hundreds of thousands of miles—what an amazing gift and bonus!*

If I max the card(s) out, I transfer the balance free to another card with an introductory zero balance offer and continue to build up the miles.

Why Southwest and not another airline that fly's internationally as well? Because I LOVE SOUTHWEST! Pick your seat, early boarding options, no bag or other upcharges. What a great business model for how to run a business—I do feel like it's all about me. And speaking of that, how can I bring some of that model into my fix and flip business?

Conclusion

In conclusion, the cost of borrowing money to finance your first fix and flip is just another expense, so don't let it intimidate you. Market yourself and your skills to several of the sources of financing I've suggested and see what happens. You may need to put together a brief business plan or prove that you are working with an experienced mentor and are therefore a good risk. Once you've got some preliminary financing commitments, compare the terms to determine which one is the best. If numbers just aren't your strength, ask your agent or an accountant friend for help. Creativity is the key to success in all of the steps of your first fix and flip!

CHAPTER SIX

WHAT TO DO / CREATING A BUDGET

In this chapter let's continue to look at the steps that will help ensure you become a successful flipper. We'll start by evaluating the physical project, and then determine the value. Next we'll look at the fix-up costs and putting our offer together. Assuming the property checks all the boxes, we'll move on to the actual fix-up process, the individual steps on ladder to success, one rung at a time.

Evaluation.

When a potential fix and flip property comes on the market, speaking of those listed with a real estate agent, you literally may only have a few minutes to determine if the price, the house, its condition and the neighborhood work for you, and then write an offer.

- Price.
- House.

  Is it a 1 bedroom, 6 bath; or a 6 bedroom, 1 bath? Functional obsolescence can often be fixed. Is it a shack or mansion, and does it fit within the constraints of your ability to purchase?

- Condition.

  How good or bad is the condition... does it only need paint and carpet, or everything, from new windows and siding, to electrical, plumbing and a new roof?

- Neighborhood.

  Good or bad, busy street or quiet, how are the neighboring properties? Physically close to you or not?

This is a quick initial evaluation—you should be able to answer most of these questions immediately.

Calculation.

We can't be buying homes at retail prices and expect to make a profit, so we're looking specifically for homes that may be listed as; fix-up, estate, foreclosure, short-sale, etc..

If you're getting daily listings from your real estate agent, make sure you're only getting those that meet your specific criteria—in fact, the agent should be hand picking those that meet your specific needs if the automated system cannot be modified.

There are a couple quick, down and dirty ways to determine initial value;

1. Zillow Zestimates; Zillow.com/how-much-is-my-home-worth

   Enter the property address and Zillow will tell you the estimated value of the home—they assume it is in good condition.

If you're looking at a fix-up home that came on the market for $220,000.00 and your zestimate comes in at $200,000.00—forget about it, it's clear there is not enough room to fix the property, list and sell the property, pay a selling commission, make a profit and pay taxes on the gain.

Don't let your emotions play a part in your decisions—the numbers are clear, they are black and white, and they are what they are… believe them and move on to the next potential deal

2. Your real estate agent.
   The best and most educated source available to you should be your real estate agent. My agents have access to a MLS / Metro list system and can run an automated value in about 10 minutes, at no cost to them or you.

And finally,

3. City and county tax records.
   Real property records are available on-line in most cities. Visit your city/ county website and click on the accessors link, from there you should be able to access the property records, enter and address and see what the current accessed value of the home is.

   This isn't the best source, as many cities tax records are not current with actual values, especially in a rapidly appreciating market—but it's another source.

With these three methods you can quickly determine if a property is a good candidate or not. If you're working with a private party on buying a home directly, you have the time and advantage of working these numbers in advance and knowing exactly what you need to buy the home for.

You'll also have the education and opportunity of being able to explain your evaluation in person and show the seller what the true market value is.

Fix-up.

Okay, time to look at the numbers.

Whether or not you're financing the cost of the house and the repair costs or not, you still need the list of repairs and the approximate costs to establish your budget. Keeping on budget is in your best interest. It may require discipline and luck, but if you plan smart, and budget wisely, you'll be in great shape to turn a profit.

Add into your budget the fix-up costs. We have a walkthrough sheet that will help you to determine those specific areas and costs at www.FixandFlip.com. Additionally, you should be walking through with your contractor for initial pricing, taking notes and verifying costs (many times I buy all materials and have them delivered to the job site, I don't need my contractor to buy them, mark them up, and then bill me for them).

Here is another down and dirty quick calculation you can use:

• Paint, carpet and light fixtures = budget $10.00 per square foot.

• All of the above plus new kitchen and baths = budget $25 per square foot.

• Complete renovation from new windows in = budget $50 per square foot.

Keeping in mind, <u>you should never, ever use these calculations</u> to determine project costs, this is just to get a rough idea. If you suddenly find yourself in a high competition situation because a desirable listing has come on the market, you can use these very rough estimates to determine whether or not it makes sense for you to bid on the house. Every home and project is different, even four of the exact same houses may have completely different needs, and requirements. Take your time to put together a though budget before proceeding.

Property insurance.

As part of your real estate contract you'll typically have an "insurance deadline" which allows you to ensure you can buy the insurance you need to insure your purchase. Try to do your homework in advance, you should check with your insurance agent, another valuable team member, to see what type of insurance they have available for a vacant home that will be going through a remodel.

I typically get my vacant property insurance through Foremost Insurance via GEICO. This policy may or may not cover fire, flood or earthquakes - be sure to check. You may have to buy those coverages separately.

Ask about different options, and make sure the insurance agent knows you intend to flip the house. If you're planning on living in the house while you flip it, your policy should be more reasonable, you'll just buy a general homeowners policy.

When rehabbing a vacant fix and flip, make sure your agent knows your intentions and is familiar with the fix and flip business. Money can be saved by getting just the right insurance, without adding unnecessary coverage.

Having insurance in place at the close, protects you and will be a requirement of your lender. Things happen, by having the proper insurance policy, you can sleep better at night.

Don't forget soft costs.

The selling costs (soft costs) are easy to forget when running the numbers but can become one of your largest expenses. Let's take a look at them;

- Real Estate Commissions
  Real estate commissions are always negotiable. This is your business and the agent you're working with consistently should be offering you his absolute best rates. You'll need to negotiate for those.

- Title Commitment

  You were provided title insurance when you purchased, and you'll have to provide this to your purchaser when re-selling. Make sure when you buy the home you request a "hold open" policy, this will reduce your title fees by 50% on the selling side.

- Pro-rated Taxes

  Taxes accrue and are paid in arrears next year. Taxes will be pro-rated during the time you owned the home and collected from you at closing.

- Closing Fees

  The title company and or attorney gets paid a fee to do the physical closing. You'll be responsible for a portion or all of these closing fees, depending on what the contract states.

- Pro-rated Utilities

  Things like water and sewer are also pro-rated to the date of closing. The closing company will escrow funds, final meter readings will be done, and you'll receive any overages in form of a refund check

Real estate commissions.

With the numbers run, it's time to write an offer. We've talked previously about your purchase contract, but ensure it is a clean as possible. It should not have a lot of inspections and contingencies, quick dates and deadlines for those that you want, plus a quick cash closing.

The offer should be written by your real estate agent or attorney. Note; if your real estate agent is paid a commission on this purchase, you should pre-negotiate a reduced sales commission on the back end. If they are earning a 2-3% commission on this purchase, perhaps negotiate a 1% over the coop commission on the back end; If it is customary that a buyer's agent makes 3% on the sale of a home, you'll have to offer this to the agent that ultimately brings the buyer, and tack on 1% for your listing agent, so 4% total sale commission on the resale of your fixed home.

As mentioned previously, if you're purchasing a house listed with a real estate agent in a highly competitive market, you may have to offer the buyer agents commission to the selling agent. This will ultimately sweeten your deal, put more money in his/her pocket, and help give your offer a fighting chance for acceptance. In this case you'll have to take care of your buyer agent on the back end of the resale.

Fix and flip deals are few and far between in many markets—give yourself every opportunity to win the bidding war on the property that works for you. Giving up a few thousand here and there can be justified with a "sure thing" back-end sale and profit.

Hold-open title policy.

When you purchase your fix and flip home, request the title company (typically the company handling the actual closing and signing) to provide a "hold open" title policy. This will save you 50% of the cost on the new title policy you'll provide the buyer of your fix and flip. This will save you anywhere from a few hundred to a thousand or more dollars. The hold open policy is cheaper, because the title search work has really already been done with the initial title policy purchase—if it's held open, they just update the policy for any changes.

Title insurance ensures the property is free and clear of all liens and encumbrances. It ensures clean title to the purchaser and will cover any issues or discrepancies down the road. It's a must for a home buyer to purchase and finance a home.

It's a winner—let the work begin.

Lipstick or extensive. Where to start and where to stop is always a great question, I tend to lean towards higher end finishes and fixtures on the fixtures and improvements on a project, vs. budget, sale and repurposed items.

Always provide a higher quality than anyone else would expect—always work harder than anyone else would expect—always make sure there is really no comparison between your finished project and the other comparable(s) on the market, and you'll always enjoy success in your fix and flip business! The details matter.

> *"A CHAMPION IS AFRAID OF LOSING.*
> *EVERYONE ELSE IS AFRAID OF WINNING."*
> —Billy Jean King

When I say higher end, I'm generally not talking about huge budget items—I'm talking about using quality fixtures and furnishings vs. budget. It doesn't have to be the most expensive, but the cheapest never works well. Stand in front of a Kohler vanity mirror at the local home depot, and then stand in front of the budget option—there's a real difference… have you ever looked in one of those "fun mirrors" at the circus? Just saying.

In should be pretty clear in your initial walk-though, and the asking price of the property, whether this is a lipstick (paint, carpet and light fixtures) project, or an extensive remodel.

The benefit of a lipstick upgrade is you can be in and out quickly! 3 weeks or less. But don't attempt to do a lipstick remodel on a project that really requires more. Nothing makes fix and flip developers look bad and will get you a bad reputation within the community quicker than shoddy, fast, sloppy, flips.

The three most important areas of your flip are… drumroll;

- Curb Appeal
- The Kitchen
- The Bathrooms

The first thing a buyer sees as they drive by the house is the exterior façade, it has to shine; Concrete, handrails, outstanding doors and lighting, cut green and mowed grass, shrubs and flowers, clean windows, shutters, possibly an awning, exterior furniture, etc.

As a real estate broker for 25+ years, the one thing I've learned is ultimately, when it comes to married couples, the wife is making the decision on which home to buy! And, the most important room to a majority of these decision makers, is the kitchen, hands down (This isn't meant to be sexist, this is just my experience). Spacious, light and bright is always the goal—if you're working with a smaller space, take the top half of a wall down and make a counter-height breakfast bar part of the space.

INSIDER SECRET: *Cabinets can be professionally refinished for about $1600.00, saving thousands. They actually remove all doors and hardware, bring the doors to their shop, and strip, prime and refinish them in any color you choose. Add some updated hinges and hardware to finish the cabinets off.*

Want to know what's in and happening in the moment? Visit www.Houzz.com and review photos and reviews of kitchens, find one you love and use it as a model for your remodel.

Adding new countertops and an under-mount sink brings you that much closer to finishing your perfect kitchen. At the moment, I'd recommend quartz countertops. Give yourself enough time to get the countertops measured, fabricated and installed; figure 4-6 weeks. Get your sinks and fixtures ready (don't skimp;

Kohler is always a safe choice), and most choices should be on hand at your local Home Depot or Lowes.

When it comes to appliances it may pay to shop around for "like new used" but don't waste a lot of time. I've shopped the world both on-line and off, scratch and dent and not, and Home Depot can typically always beat any price, offer free delivery and installation—ask when the next sale is coming, the associate will let you know and you can coordinate your purchase with that. Plus, if you're a Veteran they'll take an additional 10% off.

Reconfiguring the layout. Reconfiguration is an awesome part of how you'll increase value beyond the upgrades you make—this is the fun part! You get to use your imagination. Ponder the possibilities of what the home could become.

With age, properties can experience functional obsolesce. Remember your grandmother's home with small bedrooms and 2 ft. x 3 ft. closets? How about the homes lighting, cellar, no shower, or the narrow one car garage?

Now what are the chances you could take that tiny odd sized sewing room— punch a hole in the wall, and make that the new master bedroom closet? Or remove that wall between the kitchen and formal dining to bring in that open, light, bright new feel to the home?

I'm not a fan of additions, but I'm a huge fan of reconfiguration. Is there a new half bath possibility on the main floor?

If you have trouble initially with getting the creative juices flowing, ask your general contractor for their ideas; this is someone that is out in the field working on remodels and new home construction daily! He/she knows that if you dig out the basement floor and drop it by two feet, the basement becomes highly usable space, which will increase your value by tens of thousands of dollars.

Budgeting process.

With every job you'll create a Renovation Budget Spreadsheet like the sample below. A renovation budget spreadsheet is available for download free at www. FixandFlip.com.

Item	Material Cost	Labor Cost	Actual Cost	Notes
Permits/Fees				
Demolition				Incl. dumpster costs
Framing				
Electrical				
Plumbing				
Drywall				
HVAC				
Trim				Incl. doors & windows
Cabinets				Kitchen, bathrooms, etc.
Painting				
Flooring				
Lighting				
Appliances				
Contingency			5%	

You'll need to do your research in determining estimated costs for each of these items, depending often on the quality of the material choices. Just as an example, floor covering material and labor costs can vary widely depending on the type of surface; vinyl, carpet, tile, hardwood, veneer, etc.

I don't recommend using on-line calculators to determine costs—call for quotes and/or visit your local Home Depot and price things out. Labor costs will be provided by your contractor or sub-contractor.

You will have to know square footages for accurate pricing, so measure things out. I recommend an electronic tape measure.

I'll give you a quick example;

Item	Material Cost	Labor Cost	Actual Cost	Notes
Kitchen floor	$858.00	$564.96	_____	Vinyl $3.25 p.s.f.

You can easily call each of your sub-contractors (if you're acting as the general) and they'll provide you numbers immediately for "installing tile," for instance.

In this flooring example, your costs will not only vary depending upon the materials, but also depending upon the condition of the floor surface. So be careful and fully disclose what you have and what you'll need.

Budget for the unexpected.

I've never had a project that didn't have a surprise, so let's plan on it, prepare for it, and pray it's a little one.

"THE SECRET TO HUMOR IS SURPRISE."
—Aristotle

On a recent project we were working on, a basement floor drain was backing up. We called out our sewer guy and had the line snaked, to no avail. His snake would go out the entire length, 150 ft., and nothing, no blockage. The water would initially go down, but then slowly build back up again (we weren't really using much water on the site in general, as we were under construction).

Our next thought was to call out a sewer scope company to see if they could see anything with a camera they send through the sewer line.

You can imagine my surprise when the sewer scope company told be the sewer line was collapsed in a sink hole, underneath the middle of our street… yikes!

My first thought was "oh shit" and my second thought was "oh, under the city street—city issue." Within minutes I was on the horn with the water and sewer department explaining our situation. Of course, the city would take no responsibility, instead suggesting a leak in our line connecting to the main may have caused the sink-hole. I countered with my suggestion, that poor road fill had over time sunk, thus causing our sewer line to collapse (the chicken or the egg).

I recognized that we needed a quick solution. I was told by the sewer scope guy a plumbing company would charge $14,000.00 to $18,000.00 for the repair, but I knew there had to be a better solution.

Some months prior I had received a bid from a trenching company to re-route a sewer line at a meditation center I attended, so I called them. One day and $4800.00 later, the street was saw cut and trenched, the collapsed portion of the sewer line was replaced, new road fill was installed, a new blacktop patch was in place, and the city streets were back in business. Keep calm and soldier on.

INSIDER SECRET: *There is always more than one possible solution to a problem. Ask others for advice, you only know what you know, and others may have something you never would have considered.*

Adding a 5% budgeted contingency, based upon the total repair budget for the project, will always save you! If you're total repair budget is $85,000.00, there should be a line item "Contingency" for $4,250.00 minimum.

Roof and foundation.

It's relatively easy to visually inspect a roof and determine if there is any damage or not, but I still recommend having a roofer drive-by. In Colorado, the hail capital of the world (it feels like) we get hail storms that completely shred roofs in various parts of the city, almost annually.

A roof is a fairly expensive "surprise" that should never be one. If you have a bad roof on a property you're considering buying, particularly if it's storm damage, there is a good chance the homeowner can still turn a claim in to their insurance company. If you are considering purchasing a house with an obviously hail damaged roof, have the homeowner call his insurance company about the roof. The insurance company will send out an adjuster. Find out what the adjuster has to say about the roof. If the roof is completely shot but the insurance company won't pay a claim on it, you'll need to factor a new roof into your repair budget. Depending upon the size of the roof that could cost $10,000 or more. On the other hand, you may get lucky. If the insurance adjuster decides the homeowner is covered and the house needs a roof, that's an expensive repair you won't have to make. There might be a free roof in their future—which will now be your new roof. Always check all structures; home, garage, sheds, etc.

When it comes to foundation issues, as I mentioned previously, I won't buy a home with serious foundation issues. If you're in doubt, always call in a structural engineer or a highly reviewed foundation repair expert to access the issue and provide an estimate for repair. I've run into many structural issues in looking at deals and can't remember one that I actually purchased.

Denver, like many cities across the country has some expansive soils, especially near mountainous areas—in areas like this, be especially vigilant to potential issues. The floor can actually feel slanted, doors may not quite close correctly, cracked concrete basement slabs and the like.

Should you choose to move forward with a minor structural issue, again, find an expert who has great references and use them to repair the issue. This isn't the place where you want to scrimp. Ask for a guarantee of the work, one that will transfer to your new owner. Without a strong structural foundation, the rest of the work and house are compromised.

Lead, asbestos and mold.

The three biggest health hazards in a home are lead, asbestos and mold. Most mitigation companies handle the abatement of all three. Although each require different mitigation techniques, they can all be quite expensive. Whether or not purchasing and flipping a house with expensive environmental problems such as lead, asbestos, and mold makes sense depends upon your budget. It may cost $20,000.00 to properly rid a house of mold, but if you've been able to purchase a $500,000.00 house for $300,000.00, it may make sense. It all depends upon your budget.

When selling your remodeled home, you'll be required to disclose everything, including whether you found any lead, asbestos or mold—you'll have to disclose, and you'll have to ensure the mitigation work has been done by a licensed state approved contractor.

With mitigation companies, like all your contractors, sub-contractors and suppliers, make sure to negotiate reduced "contractor rates" (wholesale if you will). You'll develop relationships with these companies and individuals. Remind them you intend to support them exclusively for your needs, and you'll have the opportunity to refer lots of business to them via your multiple home buyers, sellers, and realtor contacts, etc.

Pest control.

Don't neglect any existing pest problems in your residential flip. Pests can include anything from mice, to roaches, to termites. Your home inspector will likely draw your attention to any termite damage the house has. Termites will require treatment by a specialized termite subcontractor. Then, any damaged wood will need to be replaced. Other pests should be handled by ordinary pest control subcontractors. Most houses have normal pest problems such as roaches or mice that may cost a few hundred dollars maximum to handle. Termite damage could potentially add thousands of dollars to your repair budget.

You probably already know the specific risks and issues in your part of the country. Ensure you're doing your due diligence and be aware of these potential problems.

HVAC.

Repairing or replacing the major systems in the house, such as HVAC, (heating, ventilation and air conditioning) can be a major expense. When you buy your flip, be sure to check the age and condition of these major systems. Experts say that they should be replaced every twelve to eighteen years.

Should you have a furnace under its life expectancy, and it looks in decent shape, have your HVAC contractor clean and service the units prior to sale. If everything is in decent shape and passes muster, then you don't necessarily need to automatically replace them because of age.

Finding older homes with furnaces and air conditioning systems thirty and forty years old is not uncommon. If your flip's furnace and air conditioning have some mileage, it's prudent to consider a replacement. Buyers will love the fact that their new home has a new furnace and air conditioning. It eliminates the what-ifs that get in the buyer's mind. If your flip still has window air conditioner units, it's prudent to put in a central system. Buyers will see window air conditioning and just keep on driving. They won't stop to look inside your flip.

New furnaces vary in price depending on the efficiency. Check with a local HVAC company and ask them about any discounts. If they know you'll be doing more flips, and referring them business, they may work with you on wholesale/contractor pricing. In a typical sized home, say under 2500 s.f. (square feet), a furnace replacement should cost under $2,000.00.

With the HVAC people on site, they can also add or replace any venting or exhaust systems should you want to include them in a room. Poor exhaust or no exhaust fans in the kitchen and bathrooms, for instance, need to be addressed. There's no sense remodeling the kitchen without making sure there is adequate exhaust.

At the tail end of the remodel, don't forget to replace all the register covers. Over the years, register covers can take a lot of abuse. Some can't even be shut. So, put on some new covers, which will enhance the face-lift of the home.

Speaking of heating and cooling, should your house have a fireplace, be sure to check the integrity of the fireplace, both inside and outside. You don't want any structural issues or any separation of the chimney and the roof. It's not likely that you'll replace the entire fireplace in a flip, although you may add a gas insert, tile over unsightly brick or stucco, replace or add a beautiful mantle, etc. Adding new tile or bricks around the fireplace gives it a fresh look without adding too much to your budget.

If the fireplace has been used, you should have the chimney cleaned by a licensed chimney sweep. Also have the flue checked to ensure safe use. Again, you can also get a fireplace insert that gives the old fireplace a modern touch.

As a reminder, some cities have banned wood-burning fireplaces due to EPA restrictions. Therefore, before sinking money into the fireplace or adding a wood burning stove, check to make sure if your city, county or state allow their use. Even some rural communities and surrounding countryside have bans in place. It's worth the time to check what rules are in place in your area.

Electrical and plumbing.

Electrical and plumbing updates and upgrades are an essential part of your fix and flip project—it pays to shop around for a smaller company or individual (master electrician) that can meet your dates and deadlines, offer big company service, at more reasonable fees.

Big electrical companies are great, and depending on their reviews on Yelp and Google, may do excellent work—but with big companies, comes big offices, big shops, lots of employees, fleets of trucks and high rates.

This isn't a fault, it's a fact of life running big companies, and it's expensive. That's why I recommend smaller companies and even individuals that are reliable, highly rated, and can service your needs in a timely manner.

There are many potential expenses when it comes to electrical;

- What is the age of the service panel, and has it been upgraded?
  Some service panels have been outlawed, they're dangerous—best to have your electrician look at this.
- Is there room in the current panel for the required upgrades?
  You'll be bringing in an entire new kitchen and baths, lots of new circuits will be required.
- Is there any aluminum wiring that will have to be pig-tailed?
  Pig-tailing outlets is a requirement in homes that have aluminum wiring.
- Is there any knob and tube wiring that will have to be replaced?
  We're talking old wiring—often bare in spots, typically in walls that contain newspaper for insulation, chicken wire and cement with asbestos.
- Is there physical access to add switches and outlets per new code?
  New code will require outlets typically every 2 ft. over a kitchen counter. And if you run into an inspector like I did, having a bad day, even your 11" piece of counter to the right of the stove, against a wall, will require an outlet. Not code required—inspector required… no sense in fighting city hall.

- Are there GFI outlets in place, or do they need to be added?
  Required to any outlet near water in bathrooms and kitchens.

Once you've toured your prospective flip house with your home inspector, you'll have a better idea of the home's electrical issues and what it might cost you to address them. Once you know what you'll need to repair and replace, you can call some electrical contractors to get estimates to add to your renovation budget worksheet.

Plumbing upgrades. When it comes to plumbing, again, there will be required upgrades as you add a possible bathroom, expand a kitchen, or even reconfigure the space within these areas;

- Is the water supply line lead?
  This may very well have to be replaced, from the street tap to the house. Lead pipes can leach lead into the drinking water and should be replaced. Trenching, removal and replacement—check code.
- Is there galvanized pipe within the house?
  Rusty, leaking, used on the original water supply? These pipes deteriorate from the inside, slowly closing off the water flow. Low water pressure should be your first clue to a problem. They should be removed and replaced—check code.
- Will a basement bathroom need to be added or reconfigured?
  We're talking about saw-cutting the concrete floor, trenching and running new drain and waste lines. Don't panic, it's done all the time, just make sure you have budgeted for it.

Your home inspector and contractor will no doubt play a huge role in helping you decide what plumbing repairs must be made in your first fix and flip. Once your home inspector has identified problems that must be addressed, your contractor can help you determine what to budget for those items.

Are permits required?

Permits, and the requirement of the same vary state by state, city by city and county by county. In Denver, CO where I've done the majority of my flips, if *you're* replacing "like with like" (taking out kitchen cabinets, putting in new kitchen cabinets, etc.) there are no permits required. New windows? No permits required. But again, check your local zoning and permitting requirements.

Permits are not that expensive and it's really a relatively painless process. It's the time delays that hurt, so plan for this step well in advance and add the estimated costs to your budget.

So are permits absolutely, positively, definitely required for everything? I'd be lying to you, and so would every other fix-and-flip contractor on the planet, if I told you I have pulled permits for 100% of my projects, 100% of the time. But everything is always done by licensed, insured contractors, and done to code.

> *"IT IS NOT ENOUGH THAT WE DO OUR BEST;*
> *SOMETIMES WE HAVE TO DO WHAT IS REQUIRED."*
> —Winston Churchill

At one point in my illustrious fix and flip career I was working on a project and we had it pretty much gutted, we had a couple of doorways cut out and widened and were working on stripping out the old tile on the kitchen floor (when I say we, I'm talking about my contractor). One afternoon I receive a call from my contractor in a sort of panicked voice; "are you sitting down" she said… my reply was, "no, why?" her reply, "the city just shut us down"… that was one of the sickest feelings I've ever had… shit!

Sure enough, after racing to the project I witnessed the "STOP WORK" order plastered on the front of the home, printed in bright neon yellow paper. The contractor working on this project was licensed, just not licensed in this particular city, so initially we mutually agreed to proceed without permits—whoops.

Panicked, I reached out to another contractor that I had used primarily for the past 20 years. He agreed to help us out by pulling the required permits, which we did the very next day, and the work proceeded.

This stop work order was a first for me. I didn't know what to expect when I went down to the city to pull a permit after the shut-down, I thought the best policy was to just come clean. When we were called to the counter I sat down and said, "I received a stop work order, and I'm here to pull the necessary permits." Without batting an eye, the clerk said "Ok, tell me what you want to do," and that was that.

30 minutes later with permit in hand I was on my way back to the project to remove the stop work order, post the permit, and get back to work.

As a final note on this subject, my lawyer told me to tell you YES. Always, always, always pull permits when they are required.

Legal fees.

The only time I really use a lawyer is when we need legal documents for a property, or to help settle a dispute with a contractor or sub-contractor.

For instance, I'd use a lawyer to draw up a "party wall" agreement if I'm doing a legal split of a duplex (buying the two units, to ultimately sell off each side individually). In this case, the party wall agreement outlines the duties and responsibilities of each homeowner in relation to the property.

If you're thinking of doing a duplex split where you live, please be sure to check with your local city and county officials to see if splits are legal in your city and county. Splits are legal in Denver but are not allowed in many of the outlying suburbs. I'm not sure why, as it would increase the value of the property, and the tax base for the jurisdiction.

INSIDER SECRET: *Using a service like GURU.com you can search for a lawyer specific to the issue you need assistance with, and lawyers will bid for the work. There is no sense in paying $250.00 to $350.00 or more per hour, for letter writing.*

That being said, if you have a serious legal or financial matter, always hire the best!

With real estate and flips, and really any area of your life, DON'T PRACTICE LAW. If you have something a lawyer should be involved in, a problem contractor, a property line dispute, review of a complicated contract, etc. it's much better to be on the side of caution. In a dispute, often, a $150 letter from a lawyer can solve an issue without going further.

The fix and flip business isn't fraught with legal obstacles, but there are times that a lawyer is helpful in resolving issues.

Let's talk about profit.

When I'm looking at purchasing a fix-up property, I want to make a minimum amount of money for the risk I'm taking on. I'm not doing this for the fun of it.

I won't risk my time and money on a project that earns me $10.00 per hour, or worse, loses money!

Here are my requirements (yours may be different);

- I'll look at a purchasing a cosmetic flip home with a profit potential of $30,000.00 or more. Again, that's me, and it may not be you—you may be thrilled with a $10,000.00 profit.
- I'll look at purchasing a home that needs a through renovation with a potential profit of $60,000.00 or more.

I try to provide myself a generous budget, so generally if one item (room) costs a bit more, or a lot more, there usually is another that can be brought in under budget.

Having a written budget in place helps you to borrow just what you need, when you need, and not borrow it (and pay interest on it) before you actually need it.

Conclusion

To conclude, determining what you will pay for your first fix and flip, what all of the repairs and upgrades will cost, and your final sales price is a crucial skill. Read through this chapter more than once and make yourself a checklist. When first considering whether or not to purchase a particular house, mentally run through every system on your checklist. Then, put pencil to paper and estimate your repair costs as accurately as possible. It's always smart to add a fudge factor. Presume that something unexpected will happen and budget extra money for it. Once you have a good idea what your repairs should cost as well as the final sales price of the house, you'll know what you can offer the seller and still make an excellent profit for yourself!

CHAPTER SEVEN

HIRING A CONTRACTOR

In this chapter, I'll teach you how to find the right contractor for your first fix and flip. The ideal contractor is hardworking, experienced, honest, reasonably priced, and communicative. Since you are new to residential flipping, along with your mentor, your contractor will be your most important instructor. Where do you find he/her?

The right contractor will be an invaluable asset for your team and your profit margin. However, choosing a truly excellent contractor may be the biggest challenge you face as a fix and flip developer.

There are many potential sources to find a qualified contractor, the #1 being a referral from your real estate agent, or possibly friends and family. In addition, good contractors can often be found by networking with other fix and flip developers, and through sources like yelp, home advisors and Angie's list.

Be certain to check all professional references before hiring a contractor to work for you. Don't just take the contractor's word about jobs he/she has completed. It's well worth your time to make a few calls, check out Yelp and Google reviews, visit some houses your prospective contractor has rehabbed if possible and check with your local city licensing authority for any complaints that may have been filed.

Other factors to consider when choosing a contractor include:

1. Is your contractor a working contractor?

   What you really want is a "working contractor," someone that will be there most every minute of every day working himself, in addition to supervising his employees and the sub-contractors. Non-working contractors are just expensive babysitters, coming and going to your job and various others. You may not see them for days.

2. How many jobs is your prospective contractor currently working?

   Good contractors, those with numerous glowing reviews on Google and Yelp, are typically busy. If your prospective contractor is currently juggling many jobs, he may be good, but unable to handle your project in a timely manner. What guarantees can he provide you that your project will take priority? This is a business for you, and time is money.

3. Is your prospective contractor currently available and for how long?

   If you've identified a good fix and flip property and are preparing to close on it, your contractor will need to walk through it quickly to produce a written estimate. Then, you'll want him to begin work the day of closing.

   If the prospective contractor is so busy that he can't get to your project for days or weeks, then don't hire him/her. Furthermore, if he tells you that he's currently very busy with projects but he can handle your rehab, how will he do that?

   The worst that can happen is that you hire a contractor who can't begin work on your project for days after he told you he was immediately available. Take the time to thoroughly question your prospective contractor on the phone or over lunch and listen carefully to what he says and how he says it.

4. How quickly does your contractor return phone calls?

   Communication is key. If a contractor isn't returning your calls promptly, then he/she is either too busy or you're just not a priority. A failure to promptly return your phone calls early in the hiring process is a warning sign for future communication.

5. Does your contractor's personality mesh with yours?

    Determining whether your personality is a good fit with your contractor's may take some time. It may not be something you can determine with an initial phone conversation or lunch. Trust your gut on this, and by the time you're done with your first project you'll know whether you'll be using them again.

6. Is your contractor licensed, bonded, and insured?

    Busy, expensive, well reviewed contractors are usually licensed, bonded, and insured, but you should never assume this, because your financial security depends upon it. Always check.

    In addition to requiring your contractor to provide proof of insurance, be certain that any subcontractors he/she use are also insured.

    The house you intend to rehab will also need to be insured during the period you own it. Because it will likely be vacant while you rehab it, ordinary property insurers probably won't insure it and you will need to turn to a specialty insurer such as Foremost.

7. How many people work for your contractor?

    Determining how many people actually work for your contractor may require a little snooping. You may need to visit a current project to determine how many workers he really has.

    Contractor size is an important consideration because large rehab projects generally require many workers. Make sure the contractor isn't fibbing about his labor force to win a job he wants.

8. Can your contractor handle all the renovations your project needs?

    Simply stated, if your contractor is unable to handle renovating all major systems in your residential flip, from the plumbing to electrical and beyond, then why use a general contractor?

Since fixing and flipping isn't a business you can run without having the right players on your team, professional people that will make the entire process run smoothly, it's important to start the evaluation process here. These are the people who will be with you through thick and thin and help you achieve your goal.

As with any team, you want to find people that are not only skilled at what they do, people who care about doing an excellent job, but also people with whom you can get along. If the chemistry is wrong, things will not run efficiently.

With professionals you can trust, you'll have the assurance that you can navigate the fix and flip terrain with confidence. The first-time flipper will find and continue to find, as time progresses that the right professionals can save you time, money and help you to sell your house at a profit.

Working with a general contractor.

Once you're decided which house is the best choice for your first residential flip, walk the house with your general contractor during your inspection period, or prior to making a written offer to purchase. A good contractor will likely be able to point out necessary repairs that you might miss. Your general contractor should be able to give you a verbal "ballpark" estimate on repairs and upgrades. You should require a written estimate from him as soon as possible.

Once your general contractor has given you an actual written estimate, then you will have a much better idea of the profit level in the project. Time is of the essence, so try to get a written estimate within a day or two of your walk through.

Your realtor can help you assess the current market value of the house once it has been repaired and upgraded, by pulling sales comparables of similar properties in the neighborhood. Once you know the potential market value of your fixed-up flip, you can determine your potential profit.

Your profit on the residential flip is the market value of the house less all rehab expenses, real estate commissions, soft costs, and your original cost for the house. Knowing the potential market value of your flip and the cost of all expenses will help you to determine what you can offer the seller for his house.

Market Value of Flip

- *Original Cost*

- *Rehab Costs*

- *Real Estae Commissions*

- *Soft Costs*

=   Investor Profit

Set a schedule with your general contractor for project completion. Include bonuses in your schedule for a quick-finish, and/or penalties for a late job (penalty clause). There are some remodels that can be done as quickly as 30 days... paint, carpet, new lighting and countertops, etc.

Your contractor should break the job down into phases of work and a specific timeline, so that everything is done in an orderly and timely fashion. Post the project calendar on site and keep your project on track. The contractor will divide up the workload and know when to start one area and move on to the next. He/she can assign the right people to the job.

Don't micro-manage your contractor if they're clearly engaged and staying within timeframes and budget, but be aware and present on the jobsite often.

If you're receiving draws from your lender on the improvements, not only do you need the list of materials and when they'll be needed, but you also need to have a list of specific tasks/jobs and completion dates. This assists the lender in knowing how well the rehab is progressing. You and your lender will know how much of the project has been completed and when the job will be finished.

To-do list, and scheduling.

You should already have a pretty through to-do list after the initial walk-though you completed with your contractor, and you have created a Renovation Budget

Spreadsheet, so let's pull out the giant calendar and start plugging in dates and deadlines.

1. Permits/Fees. *Permits can be pulled and in place prior to closing if possible.*
2. Demolition. *Everything that won't be saved; cabinets, counters, doors, popcorn ceilings, carpet, etc. (keep light fixtures in place, until they are replaced)*
3. New Framing. *Moving or adding a wall, expanding the Master Bdrm. closet?*
4. Electrical upgrades and additions. *Check code on kitchen, bath, and bedroom requirements.*
5. Plumbing upgrades/additions. *New basement bathroom / jackhammer floor?*
6. New drywall and texture. *My preference is smooth ceilings with a knock down texture on the walls—but follow the current trends (not what you love).*
7. HVAC—Heating, Ventilation and Air Conditioning.
8. Trim, doors and windows.
9. Kitchen / Bath cabinets installed. *My preference for new cabinets; IKEA.*
10. Painting. *Ceilings, walls and trim / flat paint on ceilings and walls (eggshell in kitchen and baths), semi-gloss on trim.*
11. Flooring.
12. New light and plumbing fixtures installed
13. Countertops installed.
14. Appliances.

Let's talk about the exterior;

1. Landscape demolition
2. Soffit and gutter repair / replacement
3. New Windows
4. Trim and foundation facade repairs + tuck pointing.
5. Replace lighting, mailbox and possibly doors.
6. Awning / shutter installation.
7. Paint.

8.   Landscape installation.

Based upon the realistic dates and deadlines you've entered in your calendar, print out a schedule of activities for the general contract and each of your sub-contractors.

If you're acting as the general contractor, remember, you're the guy that needs to be on-site every morning. Make sure your sub-contractors are scheduled in advance, and are on-site and working, and have the supplies and materials they need for the day. You're the orchestrator of events! You're the squeaky wheel! (The squeaky wheel gets the grease…), you'll have to schedule and remind, and remind, and remind again, all of the sub-contractors on your site.

You'll soon discover that job #1 is ensuring others are performing as they have promised, and you have scheduled.

If suddenly the framer is sick for a week, guess what, the drywall contractor is still scheduled to come in, and the project won't be ready! Don't piss everyone off—coordinate rescheduling as quickly as possible… everyone has other jobs already on the books. You may have to find another dry-wall contractor or painter if they're booked solid.

Building your team.

If you've decided to hire a general contractor for your residential flip, then your team will likely consist of you, your contractor, and your real estate agent. A general contractor should provide all of the subcontractors that you will need for your project, and they will all be under his/her direct supervision.

You'll need a clear and detailed written agreement or contract between you and your contractor so that the duties and obligations of each party are clear. Check on-line for various resources on contractor contracts, and have your attorney edit to suit your needs.

If you are acting as your own general contractor, then your team will be much larger and more challenging to manage. In this scenario, your team will consist of you, your realtor, and all of the subcontractors.

Act as a general contractor or hire one?

Most inexperienced residential flippers hire a general contractor and sort of listen and learn as they go along. This is not a bad strategy, assuming that hiring a good general contractor allows you to still make a profit on your first flip. In this case, you supervise the contractor, who is responsible for supervising and paying his subcontractors.

INSIDER SECRET: *After completing a few residential flips, you should feel that you've learned enough to act as your own general contractor—this is the goal! You don't need to have a general contractor's license to hire licensed sub-contractors and coordinate every aspect of your project.*

Acting as your own general contractor requires serious project management skills. Additionally, you'll have to find a large variety of highly skilled, trustworthy subcontractors who are reasonably priced and reliable, with great references. Once you become skilled at finding, hiring, and supervising numerous subcontractors who are reasonably priced, your profit margins will grow.

Setting expectations.

As a residential real estate fix and flip developer, you've invested an enormous amount of time and money finding the perfect house and purchasing it. You've also likely spent significant amounts of time finding well priced contractors and subcontractors with excellent references.

Before you actually begin your flip project, be clear on your expectations with your contractor and/or subcontractors so that they understand what your needs and expectations are, with dates and deadlines. I recommend actually putting these expectations in your contract or in the binding estimate they provide and going over them personally with your contractor and/or subcontractors.

"ACCOUNTABILITY BREEDS RESPONSIBILITY."
—Stephen Covey

Let your contractors and subcontractors know that you as the owner will be at the project on a daily basis. Nobody wants to be micromanaged, so it's important to strike the right tone with your supervision and involvement, but hold them accountable to the schedule and promises they have made. Your contractors and subcontractors need to know that you could stop by at any time so if they're not on the job, or workers are there not knowing what to do, you'll know immediately. The repercussions for these actions need to be clearly spelled out in your written agreement.

Unexpected problems almost always crop up when refurbishing and flipping a residence. It's not uncommon to rip out a wall and find a little bit of mold or rip up flooring and find a crack in the slab. Your contractor and or subcontractors need to understand that it is their duty to notify you immediately of any additional and unforeseen problems they discover that might increase your expenses. This expectation should also be in your written agreement.

Everything in writing.

If you've chosen to work with a general contractor, your written agreement with he/her should clearly spell out the duties and obligations of each party. Again, you can find many examples of contracts on-line, or review the contract your general has and modify it to protect your best interests. Alternatively, you can work with an attorney to develop a contract.

If you have chosen to act as your own general contractor, then you should have binding, written estimates with each subcontractor for his/her piece in the flip. Your subcontractors are likely experienced in putting together a written estimate and should have a form that they use. Read your subcontractor's binding estimate form carefully and if it favors him to heavily, consider having your attorney draft a binding estimate form with terms that favor you.

A big thing to look for with your contractor and or subcontractors is how are change orders handled? Will you be nickeled and dimed for any small deviation to the project? With any project you can expect changes and deviations from the original plan. Just make sure your contractor works with you on these changes and doesn't expect to hand you a new invoice with every minor deviation!

Contractors are somewhat notorious for overbooking themselves. Your residential flip will be progressing very nicely when your contractor and his subcontractors just suddenly disappear. Usually, the contractor is committed to another project and since he can't be in two places at one time, he's temporarily abandoned your project.

I've experienced a contractor disappearing for a day or two. Again, my motto is "the squeaky wheel gets the grease" and trust me, I can squeak pretty loud. The minute my contractor or one of the scheduled sub-contractors is missing, I'm on the phone. If you're not at the project every day, you'll never know if things are proceeding as scheduled or not.

If you're concerned about the contractor abandoning your project, have a real estate attorney write a clause that you can put into the contract which would include the circumstances under which you can consider your project abandoned by your contractor.

For example, if your contractor and his subcontractors have been missing from your flipping project for a week, then he is fired and perhaps he owes you a fine. Once a certain period of time has passed, you can hire another contractor and move forward with your project.

Selecting subcontractors.

Many fix and flip developers choose to act as their own general contractor and perhaps you're confident enough to do the same.

If you're new to the fix and flip business, obtain a detailed and exhaustive home inspection report to identify all issues that must be repaired. You'll also have to decide what upgrades the house needs so that it truly matches the high-value neighborhood sales comparables. Home inspectors can be found in a variety of ways. An excellent place to find a qualified home inspector is a referral from your real estate agent. Additionally, Internet searches for home inspectors are helpful because reviews are so readily available. Take the time to read what other people have to say about them.

If you are able, go with your inspector when he inspects your rehab project. Politely ask your home inspector as many questions as possible and take detailed notes. When he points something out, try to catch a quick photo with your cell phone. Some inspectors are even willing to give you a ballpark idea of what a repair will cost.

Of course, every home is different, but you will typically need a team of the following subcontractors:

- Demolition
- Framer / finish contractor
- Flooring / carpet. tile and hardwood
- Electrician
- Plumber
- HVAC / heating, ventilating and air conditioning
- Kitchen & Bathroom / cabinet assembly, tile, countertops

- Landscaper
- Drywall / hanging, finishing and texture
- Painting
- Windows

Be very wary about hiring your sub-contractors from Craigslist or other "classified" websites—I've been disappointed more times than not using services like this in the past. Sometimes these subcontractors simply never show up for appointments. Sometimes they'll take your deposit, but not show up for work. Sometimes they won't finish the project on time, or at all! There is generally a reason they are not working for a company. Today there are many good sources of contractors with reviews available, so skip the classified sites.

> *"IF YOU PAY PEANUTS, YOU GET MONKEYS."*
> —Chinese Proverb

Where should you find highly qualified, low cost subcontractors? YELP has typically been my go-to for finding sub-contractors—the reviews are invaluable and can save you tons of frustration with bad contractors and subs. I religiously leave both positive and negative honest reviews.

Angie's List, Home Advisor, and Thumbtack are also great sources. Just a simple search via search engines such as Google or Bing is an excellent first step. If, for example, you are seeking interior painters, you would search for "interior painters, (your city name)."

Once you have your team in place you can rest assured you're in decent shape to take the next step in your fix and flip journey.

Professional tips for working with subcontractors:
- Always receive at least three bids for every project.

- Don't assume that the highest bidding contractor will do the best job for you. Request and rely upon professional references from your subcontractor's prior clients.
- When acting as your own general contractor, ask your subcontractor for discounted or "contractor rates." Let him know that you are looking for a long term working relationship, so that you receive his/her very best rate.
- Don't assume that bigger is better when it comes to contractors and subcontractors. Larger subcontractors have overhead costs that smaller ones may not have, so they have to charge more. Look for contractors who are well reviewed, responsive, respectful, and affordable.
- Avoid paying subcontractors upfront. If your subcontractor is on a shoestring budget, then pay for his materials upfront and pay him at the end of each day for the work he's completed.

Conclusion

In conclusion, most residential real estate flippers begin their career working with a contractor who brings his own subcontractors to the job. In this way, a rookie investor gains invaluable experience. It won't be long before you'll feel confident to be your own project manager. Finding a team of hardworking, honest, reasonably priced subcontractors is challenging and time consuming, but once your team is assembled, you'll be ready to tackle any project that comes your way.

CHAPTER EIGHT

BEFORE THE FIX-UP

In this chapter you'll learn about everything you must accomplish before you actually begin the fix-up of your house. You'll need to take steps to reduce your liability in the event of accidents or injuries. You may need to evict any existing tenants or incentivize them to move. Finally, you'll have to decide what items in the house may stay and what must go. Some homes will have beautiful items you'll want to keep!

Insure yourself and your investment.

PROOF OF INSURANCE. As project manager, it's your responsibility to be certain that your contractor and subcontractors are covered by insurance. Accidents happen and when they do, you need know that everything you're working for isn't put at risk.

Require your general contractor to provide proof of insurance for him/herself and all of his or her subcontractors. If you're hiring a general contractor, they should have their own general contractor liability insurance. The insurance should cover any bodily injury or damage the firm, or its employees accidentally cause to you, to themselves, or to your property.

Most states require that a contractor has insurance as part of licensing (if you're working with licensed trades). There are generally two types of insurance:

- **Liability** which covers property damage and injuries caused by the contractor's work.
- **Workers' compensation** which provides payments to injured workers.

If your contractor is not insured, you could end up paying out of your own pocket if your homeowners policy is insufficient or won't cover the bills of an injured contractor.

Ask your insurance agent or attorney what insurance limits are appropriate. They'll be able to tell you whether your contractor and subcontractors are actually fully and properly insured. Being underinsured is almost as bad as not being insured at all.

If you are new to flipping, you should have a competent real estate attorney who has worked with fix and flip developers before, and you should always be in the process of jotting down questions to ask him or her the next time you have an office appointment. Again, I've used guru.com in the past to locate and hire an attorney—it's a great service because you can post your needs, and have attorneys bid to provide the service.

Protect yourself and your assets.

Using the right legal entity for your residential flip can significantly reduce any liability you might face in refurbishing the house or renting it out to tenants. There are four basic legal entities that can hold your residential real estate flip;

- Sole Proprietor
- Partnership

- Limited Liability Company (LLC)
- Corporation

If you simply begin your residential flipping business by yourself, then a court would likely find that you ran your business as a sole proprietor, which is fine so long as you are well insured. If you began flipping homes with a friend or family member, a court would likely find that even if you did not intend it, you were running your business as a partnership. Partnerships convey no special protections from legal liability.

Limited liability companies and corporations can convey tax savings as well as protection from liability whether lawsuits come from contractors and subcontractors or from the new owners or tenants. It's beyond the scope of this book to go into the specifics of these two legal entities, but most residential flippers, including myself, use limited liability companies (LLC's) to limit their liability and protect their other assets from any lawsuits associated with residential flipping. Some real estate investors go so far as to place each house they flip and/or rent in its own limited liability company. Speak with your attorney or CPA to see which would be the best option.

An asset, such as a home you intend to flip, when placed inside an LLC is isolated from any other assets you might own. You might have $200,000 cash in your own name, but you don't own the house you are flipping, your LLC does. If something terrible happens at the home you are flipping, the person that has been harmed, at least in theory, cannot seek redress from you personally. He/she is limited to suing the assets contained in the LLC. So, if your residential flip is worth $100,000, then his/her damages will be limited to $100,000.

There are many places on-line where you can create an LLC, places like MyCorporation.com. Conduct a Google search and you'll find many options that are considerably cheaper than using your local attorney.

Immediately after you buy.

Once you've closed on your residential flip property the next general steps include gutting the house and then making your repairs and refurbishments. However, timing is everything and there are a few chores to accomplish before you begin the interior demolition.

GETTING YOUR HOUSE VACANT. If you've purchased your residential flip at an auction, foreclosure or tax sale, you shouldn't assume that the current residents will voluntarily leave. Once you have your prospective flip under contract, it's time to figure out how you'll get the current residents to leave.

Don't think that you or someone you hire can simply gather up the belongings of the current resident and put them on the street. Doing so could very well be in violation of local and state law.

Some real estate investors offer the current residents of a prospective flip a financial incentive to go. For example, you might offer them $500.00 to 1000.00 (or more) for vacating the home and leaving it in good condition by a particular date. Again, you'll want to check to ensure this tactic is legal in your jurisdiction. Another option might be purchasing them $200 worth of boxes and offering to rent them a U-Haul truck on moving day. Generally, these kinds of arrangements are known as "cash for keys."

Prior to demolition.

Demolition (or interior gut), when done correctly, can take a few hours or a few days to complete. Be careful who you hire to handle the demolition. It should be a pretty simple and fast job when done correctly. Ideally, your contractor will handle the demo.

If you're coordinating the demolition, a couple of weeks prior to demolition day, order a roll-off dumpster. Your dumpster should be on-site, open, and ready to be filled at curbside or in the alley. Take the time to call all of the dumpster vendors in your area because prices may vary significantly.

Consider using a Bagster if space is limited. Bagster is sort of a smaller, more flexible/portable heavy-duty vinyl dumpster that you can pick up at a home improvement store.

When you use Bagster, you have somewhere to place construction debris daily and you simply make a quick call when it's full! That's it. It's simple. Bagsters are small, but they hold a lot. They don't draw attention to your project and upset the neighbors like a huge steel drop-off may.

Don't forget to figure in the costs of keeping the site clean. Your neighbors will appreciate it. Keeping things clean will keep everything in order and keep things from getting out of hand. The cost of renting dumpsters should be factored into your budget.

Be aware that neighbors will typically help you fill your dumpster with their garbage and old furniture, so don't have it delivered too early!

BLUE TAPE LABELING. If you've promised any of the interior items to friends or family, make certain they pick up their items the day you take possession of the house. Sometimes items such as cabinets or appliances may be dated, but still in quite good condition. Friends, family, and non-profits are often extremely grateful for these gifts and it helps you out, so long as they are timely in picking up what they've been promised.

With every residential flip, you'll want some items to stay and some to go. The refrigerator may date to the 1970's, but the light fixtures may have been recently updated and should be kept "as is." It's extremely important to clearly mark any items that you intend to keep with blue tape that clearly states "STAYS." It's also a good idea to walk the project with your demo crew prior to demolition and point out to them clearly what stays and what goes.

The worst that can happen is you realize after demolition that your contractor has removed and trashed all the beautiful interior entry doors you were saving! Label everything with blue tape, including the carpet, pad, baseboards and crown molding.

On the date of closing have the gas and electric transferred into your name. You may want to call the utility companies before you close to determine what will be needed, if anything, from you prior to the transfer. Generally speaking, water and sewer will be transferred into your name by the title/closing company at the time of closing.

Once again, as soon as you're able, acquire any permits that are necessary to begin work on your residential flip. If you're able to do this prior to closing, then do so because time is money!

SUPPLIES. Prepare a list of materials with your contractor or subcontractors for each phase of the project. If you're managing the project, make sure supplies are on-site well in advance. When ordering what you need, make sure the supplier has everything on your list in stock. Waiting for things on back order only delays the process.

The day after demolition, framing will begin—are you prepared?

You don't want your contractor and subcontractors on the job if all of your supplies aren't on the site. If the supplies aren't on site, then your contractor and subcontractors will simply sit around doing nothing, on your dime. Further, if you're handling supplies, the contractor will be furious if he has to sit around when he could have been on another job.

SECURITY. What about security? Once you've closed on your property and it is vacant, have a locksmith come out and rekey the locks. Get four to six copies of the keys. I personally use a lock box on the front or back door, so contractors have access to the house when you're not there. Provide one key to your general contractor, put one key in the lockbox, and keep a key with you. Put the others in a safe place, you'll need them.

In 2005 I purchased a new home. As I always recommend to my clients and fix and flip developers, we did a walk-through the day before closing. This was brand new construction. Much to my surprise, when I went into the master bedroom closet, I noticed an in-wall safe was missing, leaving a hole in the wall. As we walked around we also noticed some of the appliances were missing in the kitchen as well. We just assumed the builder was switching them out for some reason.

The builder was as shocked as we were after we called him. Turns out someone had entered the property and stolen the missing items! In all likelihood, this was a crime of opportunity. Just like criminals will walk through a parking lot trying all of the car door handles to see if any are open, some people will try to gain access to lockboxes. Keys to the house are kept in lockboxes, so if the lockbox code isn't changed frequently enough, or if it gets into the wrong hands, this kind of opportunistic crime can occur.

You're going to have perhaps thousands of dollars in inventory, supplies and equipment at your project so make sure the house is secure and well lit. Give the neighbors your card and ask them to please call you if they see anything unusual.

Property security is a big issue for contractors. In addition to property security, you should be diligent and aware of your surroundings at all times.

"SECURITY IS NOT A PRODUCT, BUT A PROCESS."
—Bruce Schneier

When I first began to flip properties, my younger brother was working on a duplex I had purchased in a somewhat sketchy neighborhood. The property was a strictly cosmetic flip. It just needed paint, carpet, refinish hardwood floors and new counter-tops.

One evening while my brother was at the property working, an unknown individual entered the duplex, pulled a gun on my brother, and robbed him! My brother initially refused and told the guy to get the hell out. When the robber hit my brother with the gun and threatened his life, my brother surrendered the small amount of cash he had. My brother never would go back to work on the property. Be smart about your surroundings!

That duplex, which I purchased for $66,000 with owner financing, rented out for $650 per side. I later sold the duplex to an investor for a nice profit. That duplex today is worth approximately $450,000.00 and the neighborhood is decent, still not fabulous, but 70% better than it was. Real estate is always a great investment!

If you plan to work in the evenings, keep the property well-lit and keep the doors locked as much as possible. There's no need to be afraid, just be aware.

BLUEPRINTS. Before you begin adding or removing any walls in your flip, determine whether or not you'll need formal blueprints created by an architect. You'll have to check with your local jurisdiction. In the Denver, CO market where I've spent the majority of my fix and flip career you don't need formal blueprints for many of the changes you'll make within the property. Simple drawings that you can do yourself work just fine.

INSIDER SECRET: *You don't need to hire an expensive architect for minor changes as a homeowner in most markets. I take my pad of graph paper, sketch out the basic outline of the floorplan, including adding the dimensions along wall lines. Now, erase those sections of lines where you'll be removing a piece of a wall and draw a dotted line where you'll be adding a new wall (could be a closet, etc.). Place a "key" (explanation of what certain colors or dotted lines, etc. mean) at the bottom of each page.*

It's best to not disturb any load bearing walls. A load bearing wall provides significant stability to the structure just like the foundation or roof. If you feel that you really must remove a load bearing wall to improve the flow of the house your contractor should be qualified to handle this. If in doubt, consult a structural engineer or architect.

HIRING A DESIGNER. Before you purchase supplies (paint, cabinets, fixtures and hardware) for your flip, consider hiring a design consultant. A design consultant can help with the interior and exterior renovations if you're not 110% confident in your design abilities. They are like a second set of eyes, in tune with the latest styles and trends.

A designer can assist you in choosing the perfect colors, the right textures, and the right surfaces, in addition to cabinets, fixtures, and window coverings. It's important that your design flows, coordinates, and works well together. You want your residential flip to be show ready, something that the buyer will relate to on an emotional level.

Don't always rely upon the designs you used in your last project. Those design choices may already be dated.

Some people don't have a keen sense of what works and what doesn't in paint, flooring and surfaces, and how to tie those altogether. Residential design is very important and sometimes neighborhood specific. For example, the inner city has much hipper finishes than the more conservative choices in the suburbs.

"THERE ARE THREE RESPONSES TO A PIECE OF DESIGN—
YES, NO AND WOW! WOW IS THE ONE TO AIM FOR."
—Milton Glaser

Granite countertops, designer tile, top of the line appliances and custom lighting can be very expensive and may be right for some projects, but not all. Remember to keep the neighborhood in mind when making your choices—don't over improve the project or finishes.

Although buying a house is serious business, it does boil down to an emotional decision. Does the house inspire the buyer? If a buyer likes the interior and exterior "look, feel and design" of the home, the things that make it a warm and inviting place, they'll imagine themselves living there.

In the buyer's mind, they envision a lifestyle for themselves and their families. With careful thought and planning, you can provide them their dream.

As a final thought, there are lots of magazines and websites like Houzz.com that offer beautiful ideas in home finishes, décor and design. I use them myself to help with design and fixture choices. You don't have to have a designer on the team if you trust (and others have commented positively) on your design choices. A project should never be finished with "your favorite things," it should be finished with the latest market trends.

Conclusion

In conclusion, you may never have guessed the many important tasks you must accomplish before you ever begin actually refurbishing your house. You are the project manager, but some days you may feel more like a choreographer or a juggler! There is excellent money to be made in residential flipping, but it must be done correctly, and tasks must be accomplished in a logical sequence to ensure success!

CHAPTER NINE

REFURBISHING YOUR RESIDENTIAL FLIP

In this chapter, I'll teach you exactly how to progress through refurbishing your residential flip. You'll learn crucial information such as what to tackle first and why. In addition, I'll teach you how to handle all of the debris that naturally results from flipping, and how to add value to your flip through creativity. Finally, I'll show you how to make friends and allies of your neighbors, recruiting them to be your eyes and ears.

Supervising the sequence of repairs.

If you're acting as your own general contractor, you must show up at the site and check the progress of the work daily! *You* must manage the site. It's your money and your time. If you're not on site daily, you lose control of the situation.

Beginner home flippers might wonder where to begin the project. Do you start outside or tackle the interior first?

Always leave the outside for last but weave it in as necessary. If your painter has finished painting the interior, it makes sense to have him paint the trim while still on the job vs. rescheduling. Other outside projects to schedule and supervise include the roof, gutters, doors and shutters, lighting, landscape, fencing, etc.

*"ORGANIZATION IS WHAT YOU DO BEFORE YOU DO SOMETHING,
SO THAT WHEN YOU DO IT, IT'S NOT ALL MIXED UP."*
—A. A. Milne

ON TO TASK #1

STRUCTURAL. Any projects that are structural in nature such as a leaky, worn out roof, leaky plumbing or foundation repairs, and exterior doors that cannot be secured, should be addressed immediately after demolition.

A bad roof must be replaced prior to any indoor repairs or improvements, as rain or snow could cause the roof to leak, ruining any indoor improvements you've made.

Plumbing in terms of replacing pipes inside of walls or trenching basement floors should happen at this stage. Any plumbing leaks should also be prioritized. Leaking water can destroy any improvements you've made and cause mold to grow. Maybe your licensed inspector uncovered some plumbing issues below the foundation of the house that must be addressed.

Finally, make sure any access points to the house can be secured.

FRAMING. At some point, you may need to make a decision about where and how to open up some space in your residential flip. When you've finished the demolition, structural, and rough plumbing stage of your residential flip, it's now time to address any framing issues including walls and windows.

If the kitchen, dining room, or living room is too small, think about relocating or tearing down a wall, or possibly opening half. Make sure it's *not* a load bearing wall. Your contractor can help you with that.

Older homes have smaller rooms and are more compartmentalized. This style isn't really well suited for modern families. If you can't envision a new layout, talk with your contractor to see how you can create a flow to the house that will give that added space. Many times, a simple change of use on the interior can bring a completely fresh look and feel to a home, and it may bring a higher price.

With properties of any age, you sometimes see "functional obsolescence." This can primarily be found in much older homes where main floor bathrooms are absent, or the kitchen is tiny. The bedrooms may be too small with no closets or the home is just plain dark, with many rooms and a maze of hallways. The great news is walls come down easily!

In the core of the city where I live, there are many turn of the century homes. These tend to be handsome and beautiful structures with interiors that just don't meet the needs of modern couples and families. I bought a beautiful, very small brick Tudor in a spectacular neighborhood some years ago. The seller had purchased the home for their son who tragically died in a car accident.

The interior of the house was cute, but small. The home had a one car attached garage which could have easily been finished and added to the square footage. In addition, it had a brand new oversized two car garage on the alley.

The value for this home and neighborhood was really as a "scrape." Small homes are scraped, and new larger, more functional properties are built on the lot. In a few years, that would probably be the result. So, I decided on a minor remodel.

I took out a kitchen wall between a very tiny dining area that was part of the living room. I added a bar-top with seating. Now the living, dining and kitchen areas appeared larger and brighter.

Next, I moved part of the living room wall back into a larger bedroom, thus expanding the depth of the living room. I added some glass block to "let the light shine," and added a ¾ bath behind the glass block portion of the wall. Then I added a little paint, trim, light fixtures, and some new carpet in the partially finished basement and ta-da!

You don't have to spend a fortune over-improving a home. I'm not suggesting a shoddy fix and flip. Shoddy fix and flips happen occasionally, and they make us all look bad! A quick flip is fine, and quality is always the best policy.

On this little Tudor, I netted a handsome $120,000.00 profit. There is now an $850,000.00 home on this lot… my little Tudor remodel is in Tudor heaven.

ELECTRICAL. Now it's time to tackle the electrical systems. Your detailed home inspection should have indicated whether or not you'll have re-wiring to do, a panel to upgrade, or just adding some GFI outlets. Of course, it's imperative that all electrical wiring is up to the latest code requirements for everyone's safety. Your licensed electrical contractor will guide you through the recommendations vs. requirements.

Absolutely nothing says "antiquated" more than old fixtures and electrical outlets. All switches and outlets should be replaced, shiny and new.

Don't overlook outdoor lighting to improve curb appeal. A well-lit home will be a safer and more inviting home. New lighting fixtures will give your residential flip a whole new look and feel for a relatively modest amount of money.

PLUMBING. Truly major plumbing issues such as excavating pipes, replacing pipes inside of walls or trenching basement floors were handled right after demolition. Now is a good time to rough in all the plumbing that will be needed to handle the new kitchen and bathrooms.

DRYWALL & TEXTURE. Next, move on to the drywall in the house and bring on the sheet rock crew. It's time for them to come in and repair and texture any cracks or holes and hang new sheetrock. Taping and mudding will be done the same day, with sanding and re-mudding done over the next few days, followed by texture. They can even hang wallpaper in your main floor half bath or entry. You'll be amazed at how the house is starting to look at this point!

DOORS/TRIM. Unless they are historic, replace all doors and hardware. If re-hanging the original doors, you may need to repaint or refinish them. If you don't replace the original doors, think about adding some great new hardware.

Fix or replace cracked trim and frames in doorways. Speaking of doors, add new exterior doors, if necessary. This will enhance the curb appeal and the safety of the house, in addition to insulating it.

WINDOWS. You may want to replace old, energy inefficient and foggy windows (windows where the thermoseal has broken). Replacement windows are a great selling feature. They improve the looks of the house more than you might imagine. In addition, they can significantly reduce cooling and heating bills, and are really not that expensive. You should be able to replace windows for about $400.00 per hole. That's all in—tear out and new installation of a good quality window.

It always amazes me when contractors use the cheapest of anything! There is a new $800,000 pop-top in my neighborhood. They've installed windows in the home that my window person would never let me use in a flip! He's told me they are the worst windows money can buy.

I never use products in a property that I would not install in my personal home. In fact, my goal is to delight the homeowner. "Under promise and over deliver," that's my motto!

Don't forget to replace damaged or missing screens, even if you're not replacing the windows. Be sure to replace any broken, cracked, or missing glass in doors and windows. Then ensure that everything is operating as designed.

KITCHENS & BATHROOMS. After the electrical system and plumbing has been updated, it's time to work on kitchens and bathrooms. Kitchen cabinets + bathroom vanities, mirrors, and medicine cabinets should be on-site and ready to install.

White is always a safe choice for kitchen cabinets, but I like to push the envelope with kitchen design. My last kitchen had white upper cabinets and walnut lowers, with quartz countertops with a waterfall. The waterfall is where the kitchen countertop continues down the side of the cabinets on an exposed end! Stunning!

TILE FLOORS. Now it's time for those kitchen and bathroom floors to be installed. This is another area where a designer can come in handy if you don't have the design gene. Once again, I advise that you search sites like Houzz.com for kitchen and bath tile specific design ideas and photos. You'll find hundreds of possible tiles, patterns and designs.

If you plan to install white cabinets, search specifically for kitchens with white cabinets and you'll see what materials are being used for flooring, countertops and backsplashes.

I like neutral tile for the floors, choosing something that is not too trendy, so it won't be dated in 3 to 5 years.

PAINT. I think very highly of Benjamin Moore paint, but you and your contractor may make other choices for your flip. No matter what brand of paint you buy, knowing the various kinds of paint finishes will help you to make the right decision for the interior of the house. Remember, keep it neutral, we're not using your favorite blue!

When it comes to things like paint…you don't have to buy the best, but with some big-box stores' most popular brand, you'll have to paint everything twice due to poor quality. "Do it right and do it once!"

Even with the best of paint and professional painters, the results will only be as good as the surface is clean. The cleaner the painting surface is, the better the results will be. Once the clean-up is done, the painters are ready to start.

When the painters finish inside, get them started on the outside of the house. Just like with the inside, you need to make sure the house is clean and free of debris and any peeling or chipped paint. Ideally, the painters should power-wash the exterior surfaces that will be painted.

I recommend using all latex paint, flat on walls and satin or semi-gloss on the trim.

First time residential rehabbers need to know a little bit about reflectivity in paint and each finishes' characteristics.

Let's look at the individual finishes to determine the best application for them. The four basic finishes are:

➤ Flat. Is non-reflective. It hides imperfections in the drywall (bonus) and is best used on walls and ceilings. I use it in every room outside the kitchen and baths.

➤ Eggshell. Eggshell has a slightly higher reflectivity than flat. It's more washable and is an excellent choice for the bathrooms and kitchen.

➤ Satin. Satin has more luster than eggshell and washes easily. This is best used on trim.

➤ Semi-gloss. Semi-gloss is shiny and very washable and is another excellent choice for trim, doors and millwork.

When in doubt, talk to the professionals at your local paint store. They understand the paint qualities, best uses, and most affordable options for your project. Don't forget to ask for a contractor discount!

Don't cut corners on the paint—if you buy cheap paint, you'll paint it twice.

FLOORING. Whether it's refinishing the hardwoods (Choice #1), adding some new carpeting or some other type of flooring such as laminate, save this upgrade for last. This will keep your new flooring as beautiful and pristine as possible because your subcontractors won't be walking on it as much. Once it's done—cover it!

While you're replacing the carpet and refinishing or installing a new hardwood floor, this is a wonderful time to check on the condition of the subfloors, particularly around sinks and water sources. If the floors are spongy or mushy, they need to be replaced. It's easy to do it now.

When replacing flooring in the kitchen or bathroom, you might have quite a time getting up the old flooring, depending upon how and when it was installed. No matter what it takes, it's best if you can remove the original flooring. The option would be cement board on top of the old, which would cause a tripping hazard entering the kitchen or bath.

FIXTURES. Fixtures include door hardware, lighting, cabinet hardware, faucets and more.

Buying door hardware (knobs, deadbolts, etc.) at Home Depot is a smart move once you've decided on a finish. The selection is broad, the service is great, and it's easy to pick up another and or exchange/return an extra.

I always buy cabinet hardware online. You can save hundreds of dollars buying your cabinet hardware online vs. buying it local. Small details like cabinet hardware can make your kitchen and bathrooms "pop" or not. Trust me, a fantastic knob or handle can be enough for someone to fall in love with your property.

When purchasing sinks and faucets, I always look for high quality. I almost always choose Kohler at Home Depot or Lowe's.

A fantastic light fixture is another item that can really show off a room. I recently installed a gold starburst chandelier with candle light bulbs, framed in black, and hanging on a gold chain. It's the first thing you notice when walking in the door. How important do you think that is?

Lighting can be super expensive, but you don't have to spend thousands of dollars. You can literally save hundreds of dollars at sites like Wayfair.com and Houzz.com, for designer lighting without the designer prices. At Wayfair you can sign up for contractor pricing and you'll be assigned a representative that will hand analyze, and typically lower the price on any item you'd like to purchase.

COUNTERTOPS. Currently, quartz appears to be the hot item of the day for countertops. I really love the look, feel, and clean designs of quartz. If you have an IKEA nearby, you can check out quartz countertop samples or check out Home Depot or call your local countertop company and they'll gladly drop some by your site.

I've used quite a bit of white subway tile for the backsplash (It's hard to go wrong with this option), although this is also a great area to make a statement and bring in some color.

BASEMENT. Don't forget the basement! That extra square footage could be a great selling point. Occasionally, basement ceilings can be too low making the space cramped and claustrophobic. I've seen people discuss lowering the basement floor (lower the floor = added headroom), but unless you're into a million-dollar renovation you probably don't have room in the budget.

There are ways to still make the basement appear taller and give it some pizazz; Add a great new plank vinyl "hardwood look" floor, recessed lighting makes the ceilings seem taller, and possibly a floor to ceiling barn door to separate or access a space (the tall door adds to the feel of height).

Basements are ideal candidates for adding additional rooms, another bathroom, a home office, or even a bedroom (which will require an egress window, about $1600.00).

Although adding extra rooms to your basement can add to the budget, it will also add to the desirability and resale value of the home.

If there is no room in the budget to refinish the basement, dust all the cobwebs off the rafters, the ductwork, the pipes, and consider adding lighting, painting, concrete block walls, and a cement floor. A coat of paint will brighten up a normally dark space.

Attics can also be great spaces, if they are redone. You could create a master suite in the attic or even add a bath adding value to your home. Adding a skylight will make the space bright and inviting. A tiny three-bedroom home will suddenly get a fourth bedroom and a bath.

EXTERIOR. Paint the garage, inside and out. Be consistent. Make it shine. You don't have to go all out but applying fresh paint that matches the house is a great touch. Add some trim and wash the garage windows, inside and out. Clean the inside of the garage as well.

Paint the garage floor, if necessary, after you seal any cracks. Adding a few shelves, hangers, and a pegboard will give it the boost it needs to please any homeowner, especially one who has a lot of tools. Additional lighting (nice bright LED lighting) and a workbench, space allowing, will be an oasis for any handyman. You can even throw in some bike racks, budget permitting.

Add some automated carriage lights outside so that the garage area will be safer at night and look terrific!

Good neighbor policy.

Throughout all of the work stages, including the demolition and all the jobs involved with fixing your flip, don't forget the neighbors. Be friendly and maintain open communication with them. Take the time to get to know your neighbors. Be sympathetic to them and understand what they're going through. It's not only about you.

"LOVE YOUR NEIGHBOR AS YOURSELF,
BUT DON'T TAKE THE FENCE DOWN."
—Carl Sandburg

The neighbors are required to put up with an increase of noise, activity, and traffic for ninety days while you turn this house into something special. Give them your card and ask them to notify you if they have any questions or concerns— better them to call you then to have them calling and complaining to the city. Additionally, let them know if they see anything suspicious, night or day, they should feel free to contact you.

Your neighbors may know people that would be interested in buying your house. When you keep the communication lines open, you'll create a good impression in their minds, and keep them and the neighborhood happy. Who knows, you may develop lifelong friends in the process that can only help you in the flipping business.

Conclusion

In conclusion, there is a logical sequence to follow when you are refurbishing a residence for profit. For example, it's far better to paint the walls before installing new flooring because you might splatter new paint on brand new flooring. However, you shouldn't paint the walls until you've decided whether that wall stays or goes. First time flippers need guidance and education and that's why I'm here!

CHAPTER TEN

AFTER THE RENOVATION

In this chapter you'll learn what you'll need to accomplish after your renovations are complete. From your final walkthrough, to passing that final building inspection and a detailed cleaning, plus possibly staging, that will make your home irresistible!

Pay attention to every detail.

TOUR AND INSPECT. Congratulations! The heavy lifting is done, and the renovation appears to be complete. It's now time for a thorough walk-through of the house making a "To Do List" of anything that needs touching up or finishing.

It's likely that you'll find mostly trivial things and some loose ends that need to be handled. Whether it's removing blue tape or discovering that one light switch not working, these are the important finishing touch details you must accomplish before putting your home on the market.

You've spent a lot of time and money refurbishing your house. Don't quit before the job is truly complete.

Check for any nicks, scratches, or other flaws in walls, carpeting, countertops, etc. Even though workers are careful about moving about while they work, bumps and nicks can happen. Touch them up and move on. Take your time and really scrutinize every room in the house. Don't rush it. Look carefully!

If you've installed a new HVAC system, then your HVAC tech should have checked it to be certain that it works properly. Don't just assume that everything is okay. Check your new HVAC system out yourself by adjusting the temperature with the digital thermostat to make certain the air conditioning and heat operate correctly.

Once the new kitchen appliances have been installed, double check to make certain they are working correctly... is the ice maker making ice? Run the hot water to be certain that the hot water heater is working. Does the hot water knob actually turn on the hot water? Do the same for the oven and stove. Visually inspect your appliances to make certain they are clean.

At the end of all of the renovations, your electrician will make his final pass through the house installing switch plates, outlet covers, final light fixtures, etc. His goal it to make certain that everything is finished perfectly.

Your contractor will go through the house installing doorknobs, locks, shower doors, and making sure all are functioning correctly.

"THE ROAD TO SUCCESS IS ALWAYS UNDER CONSTRUCTION."
—Arnold Palmer

The focus now moves outside to ensure gutters and downspouts are draining properly and are not clogged. If they need to be replaced, this is the time to do it. Also make sure that the downspout drain slopes away from the house so that water doesn't collect and seep against the foundation wall.

Conducting the final walk through.

Replace or add smoke and carbon monoxide detectors in the house on all levels as required. The specific requirements for the location and number of smoke and carbon monoxide detectors will likely vary with location. You may need clarification on this issue, so check your local regulations.

Smoke alarms must usually be near every sleeping area. One alarm is mandatory in each area, and the alarm must be in the egress path from the doorway. Smoke alarms are also required on each level of the house. If you have new construction, the alarms must usually be hard wired to the primary power source in the house, with a mandatory battery backup. Carbon monoxide detectors are usually required in or very nearby each bedroom.

Finally, we'll have the house professionally cleaned. Wash the windows inside and out. Make them sparkle, even if they're brand new. Clean the interior cabinets, countertops, and appliances to make them shine. You want everything to be polished and looking radiant for the prospective buyers.

Final city inspections.

It's not over until the fat lady sings. It can be nerve wracking waiting for the final approval from the city building inspector. Even though you hired the best people for the job and you've passed inspections along the way, you still worry whether the house will pass the inspector's final inspection. The inspector will be viewing your house from an objective viewpoint, which is different from the emotional viewpoint your buyers will have.

INSIDER SECRET: *When it comes to the final inspection I always meet the city inspector. Typically, at this point you don't have any contractors left on site, and it's great for you as the owner to walk-through for the final. It's great to listen, learn and build rapport.*

During construction as rough-in and final inspections are called by the specific trades, I never show-up for the inspections. The contractors / sub-contractors know these inspectors and know what they are looking for... stay out of their way.

Inspection fine points.

We've stressed all along that when renovating houses, you need to have a plan and you must stick to it. The most common reason renovated homes fail inspection is that the flippers, and/or the contractors didn't stick to the approved plan.

ELECTRICAL. Electrical renovations are an excellent example of how a failure to stick to the plan can cause problems. All of the electrical changes and renovations were included in the original plan. However, changes during renovation, such as failure to install an outlet, may cause problems. This is a red flag for the inspector, especially in kitchens and baths where a specific number of electrical outlets in specific areas are required.

STRUCTURAL. The inspector will be examining the structural components of the house. These include support beams, headers, roof, and foundation. The inspector will make sure that the beams and headers are structurally sound. His main concern is safety because structural problems can lead to a building collapse.

He'll also be looking for cracks, holes, or other penetrations/issues that may affect the structural integrity. Holes for wiring or cabling are normal and not a concern, but other issues may be cause for alarm.

CLEARANCES. The final inspection will include clearances in the home. The purpose of inspecting clearances is to prevent house fires. The inspector will be making sure that flammable materials are the correct distance away from heating elements.

The inspector will examine the clearance between fireplaces and any wooden surrounds. He'll also consider cook surfaces and their distance to wooden cabinets and the overhead exhaust fan.

It's the inspector's job to be a final set of eyes upon the project, ensuring the safety of future inhabitants. The inspector, of course, is the true expert on building codes.

SAFE EGRESS. The ability of future residents to escape quickly and easily in the event of fire is a huge area of concern. Thus, one of the inspection points that has multiple building codes attached is safe egress. Safe egress from the house for future inhabitants involves windows and doors. Check new windows to ensure that they open properly and meet accessibility requirements.

If you put in a large picture window in the bedroom, that's not a problem if you have another window in the bedroom that opens to code standards for safe egress. Basement windows must be large enough to provide safe egress as well.

Safe egress also includes stairway parameters, railings, and door hardware operation. You'll be glad you checked that before the inspection. These codes are necessary for resident safety in an emergency when it's critical to leave the house quickly.

In Colorado, the stairway riser height can't be more than 7 ¾ inches. Tread depth must also be considered. The depth must be a minimum of 10 inches. Even the variation between steps is regulated. A seasoned contractor will know these parameters. In new construction, the inspector will make sure the contractor followed the stairway safety parameters. However, some issues that don't meet current code may be "grandfathered" in.

If you are acting as your own general contractor and supervising the work, it's important your licensed subcontractors adhere to all the code requirements specific to your city and state.

On the last duplex project I renovated in Colorado, the handrails going down into the finished basement failed inspection. The inspector noted that a fireman walking down the stairs could get his gear hooked on the unfinished handrail end. In order to bring the handrails up to code, we had to add a 90° finished end from the handrail to the wall, at the top and bottom of each handrail.

DOORS AND WALLS. Doors and walls are also critical components of the structural integrity of the house. The inspector will be checking them closely. Typically, doors must be able to be opened from the inside and they must be a minimum of 32-inches wide.

In certain cities your inspector will be checking hardware such as connectors, hold-downs, moment frames, (an assembly of beams and columns that are rigidly bound) and fasteners. All of these components provide stability, particularly in times of earthquake or upheaval.

HVAC AND PLUMBING. Some states require your HVAC contractor to verify the efficiency of air systems within the home. He may also be required to certify that the duct system is sufficiently airtight.

Your inspector will check all plumbing fixtures. Depending upon your state, water usage may be regulated. These regulations may be stringent, if you live in states like California. On a side note, there may be discounts and rebates available for high efficiency items.

Some states have regulations that dictate how many gallons per minute a showerhead uses, while other states dictate the maximum amount of water a toilet can use per flush. Sink faucets may also be regulated in this way.

EXTERIOR. The final inspection isn't just limited to the interior of the house. The inspector will make sure that all outside plugs have ground fault circuit interrupters or GFCIs to prevent accidental electrocution. Bathrooms, kitchens, bars, and garages must have GFCI plugs anyplace there is a potential for water.

MISCELLANEOUS. In some states, you may be required to prove that you recycled a certain percentage of debris. The form for this is the green waste disposal form. It will prove that you have utilized disposal sites that are approved in the jurisdiction.

Depending upon state law, other forms may be mandatory such as insulation forms which verify the use of the correct insulation types on floors, ceilings and walls.

To summarize, your city, county and state will have its own set of regulations and codes. They may seem cumbersome on the surface when trying to deal with them. However, they are in place for our safety.

It's important to know the regulations and do the job right. Once you move on to your next flip, the permits, rules, codes, and regulations will become second nature to you.

Final payment.

Your last payment to the contractor should coincide with the satisfactory final walk through by the city, and final signature on your permit. If your contractor has completed the job to your satisfaction, then it's time to release the final payment in exchange with an affidavit and agreement.

Affidavit and agreement.

When you sell your rehabbed house, the title company will require a "Final Affidavit" from the general contractor stating that there are no unpaid bills to any suppliers or subcontractors.

When the contractor has completed all work on the project, he/she will fill out an affidavit stating that all of the materials and work for the job have been paid for and that the work is completed. He/she signs the affidavit in the presence of a notary attesting to the completion.

The affidavit will verify that everything has been paid in full. The contractor must deliver the notarized affidavit prior to closing.

Make sure you're aware of any unpaid balance and be prepared to write a final check. Once the affidavit has been delivered to you, the contractor can sue for any unpaid balance, if you fail to pay.

Any warranties/guarantees that you have from the outset of the project should be placed in a folder, to be given to the buyer at closing.

Conclusion

In conclusion, never forget that you are the project manager. Even if you have hired the best contractor and subcontractors, you must still double check their work to be absolutely certain that it is perfect and will pass inspection. If you handle every detail correctly, the house will sell itself!

CHAPTER ELEVEN

PREPARING FOR THE SALE

In this chapter, we'll talk about everything you need to know to prepare to sell your renovated home. From staging the house to make it a home, to fine tuning the exterior and working with the photographer to ensure magazine quality prints.

It's now time to stage your residential flip to create that "Wow!" factor. You might hear real estate agents refer to it as making a house really "pop."

The purchase of a residence can be a highly emotional experience. Staging is about ensuring that your prospective buyers fall in love with your house the minute they walk in the door. They can actually visualize themselves living in this new perfect space!

Three items in preparation for listing the house:

1. Have you staged the house with the appropriate furnishings and accessories?

   You've come this far, it's not worth skimping on the staging to save a few bucks. Bad staging is worse than no staging at all. According to a recent article at the National Association of Realtors ® "Realtors® believe that buyers most often offer a 1 to 5 percent increase on the value of a staged home. Additionally, 22 percent *of Realtors® representing sellers and 16 percent of Realtors®* representing buyers said the increase is closer to 6 - 10 percent!

2. Have you given sufficient thought and effort to curb appeal?
   A beautiful, elegant, sophisticated, and uncluttered appearance on the outside suggests the same on the inside. If your exterior isn't excellent, your prospective buyers may never even stop their car to look inside the house!

3. Have you or your agent hired a professional photographer so that you can post magazine quality photos online?
   Most commerce is conducted online today, at least at first. Your online presence must be professional and beautiful, and it begins with excellent photos!

Staging.

Staging the home is a critical phase in the flipping process. All the remodeling is done, and the house is sparkling clean. Now it's time to create a beautiful, picture perfect image that will capture the hearts of buyers.

Why is staging so important?

Simply put, with all the competition for buyers today, taking the time to stage the house and show off its attributes is essential. Yes, you can even do it on a budget. You may be tempted to forgo the additional expense of staging, but in the long run, it will hurt you when you sell.

Staged homes sell faster, give the buyer a better picture of the functionality of the home, and set the buyer's imagination into motion. A bare house, even if it's freshly remodeled with shiny new appliances, will not elicit the kind of emotional response you're looking for from a buyer.

When a buyer looks at a house, particularly an empty one, they're wondering if this space will work for them or not. When you take the time to stage the house, you're showing them the wonderful possibilities of living here.

Having chairs, a sofa, and even a big screen TV in the family room helps your buyer to really get the picture! They superimpose themselves into the setting. That's when their imagination kicks in and they begin to seriously consider buying the home.

Yes, staging is an expense, but one well worth it. Costs usually vary from $900 to $1800 a month depending on the style you choose. This is the price for furnishing an entire house, including accessories.

For this important marketing strategy, enlist the help of a designer or a professional stager. Ask your real estate agent for a referral or two. Make sure you've viewed the stager's photos or other staged properties before hiring—the style and furnishings must match your home and neighborhood.

> **INSIDER SECRET:** *Some cities have staging stores where you can rent furniture and accessories for your flip. My real estate agent has a great eye for design and stages my fix and flips! I generally pay him a bonus for this service, but it's not required—this is just the dedication and quality service he provides.*

If you're going to do it yourself, search google for staging stores in your area. Often, the stores have "In House" experts who can pull the whole staging process together. This is particularly helpful if you don't have a real design sense. It's worth the expense to have the pros handle this pivotal point.

Working with a designer will ensure you're choosing the right furniture for your style of house. They will be more objective than you are about the right piece to fit in a certain room. From eclectic to traditional or even trendy, a stager will know the latest styles and furnishings that will transform your empty flip into a fully furnished oasis.

The size of the furniture also matters. Too small or too large a couch will detract from the room. A huge sofa will dwarf the room, making buyers feel the space is too tight. Small sofas in a large room make the room look unfinished and give the buyer a sense that something is missing. Appropriately sized pieces present a positive picture of the room.

Although you've painted your house with neutral colors that most people will appreciate, the staging process is the time to introduce wonderful colors into the house, from decorative pillows, to towels, rugs, pottery and even paintings.

Some stagers bring in gorgeous plants from local nurseries and florists to add not only a splash of color, but also a delightful fragrance. Candles also add great color and scent.

By creating a cozy environment, the buyer will easily envision him/herself living in your house. Each room, tastefully furnished, will open their eyes to the possibilities the house offers.

Some rooms in the house carry more weight with buyers and it's important to make sure the key areas of the home are staged perfectly. The kitchen, of course, is the heart of the home. Put out a basket of fruit, cut flowers, countertop appliances, canisters, and décor. If the kitchen has an eat-in area, be sure to stage it. Dress it up by setting the table with great dishes, glasses, and silverware. At most staging stores, you can get all the trimmings to make any table look as elegant and sophisticated as any magazine cover.

If you'll be staging homes in the future, don't be afraid to buy and reuse items that can easily be packaged and hauled—artwork, towels, decanters, pottery, etc. My real estate agent has done this. Even with fully lived in properties, he fluffs!

In the dining room, take things to a more formal level. When buyers come in, they'll see an extraordinary table set for a dinner party. They'll imagine family dinners and holiday get-togethers. Then, they'll start thinking "this is my home."

Stage the house to look comfortable and inviting and keep the colors gender neutral, even in the bedrooms. This will appeal to more buyers and allow them to use their own imaginations. However, if your house has specific features, highlight them so that they stand out by using bright colors in that area that will draw the buyer's attention.

If your flip has several bedrooms, consider staging one room as a home office complete with desk, a comfy office chair, computer, and perhaps a love seat or chair. This will appeal to any professional!

Keep the thermostat set appropriately for the season. You want the house to feel cool in the summer and toasty in the winter. If a buyer is uncomfortable, they won't stay long enough to appreciate the house, and their interest in the property will wane.

Use essential oil decanters or a few drops of vanilla or cinnamon on a warm cookie sheet in the oven during an open house. The smell of cinnamon is very soothing, and it makes people think of home.

Curb appeal.

Once the inside of the house is perfect, focus upon curb appeal.

Sprucing up the yard, removing or trimming bushes, and adding focal points such as a new front door, shutters, lighting, a fountain, or shrubbery will add a great deal to the curb appeal.

It's said that for every $1000 you spend on landscaping, you'll get $10,000 in return! That puts things into perspective.

A well-landscaped lawn will invite prospective buyers. It will frame your house and draw the attention of people to the front door. There's nothing like a good looking, orchestrated landscape design that leads to an inviting front door.

If the front door itself isn't what it could be, you can turn it into something spectacular for very little cost. Perhaps you could add new paint or change the front door hardware? A brass knob, doorknocker, and a kick plate will create a wonderful transformation! Adding a modern, solid glass storm door or an awning will liven up the entrance. Light the walkway leading up to the door and upgrade the lighting by the door.

The mailbox is often overlooked. Replace a tired, old mailbox with something new that adds to the entryway. Also, change out the house numbers for some great stainless numbers that will be easily seen from the street. You don't want the address to be a secret!

Get rid of old doormats and replace them with something fresh and beautiful.

Pay attention to every single detail around the outside of the house. If the porch has loose or cracked concrete or boards, repair or replace them and repaint. Should your flip have siding that's in good condition, get it power-washed and looking its best. If the house has shutters, fix, paint, repair, or replace them. Should the house lack shutters, consider adding them—great heavy-duty plastic shutters are available on-line, very reasonably priced. Even consider new garbage cans and perhaps a metal holder. Those small touches stand out in buyers' minds. Be certain to remove any bird's nests, wasp or hornet nests.

Trim the trees as needed. Overhanging limbs block the view of the house and can obstruct the walkway. They can also be hazardous. Remove and replace any juniper/evergreen bushes and replace brown patches or spots. Fill in any empty spaces and balance the look of the home. Keep it level. Keep it simple. Keep it sharp!

Be sure to pull all weeds and remove dead plants. Depending on the season when you'll be flipping, add new plants that will brighten up the yard. If it's mowing season, be sure to keep the property mowed and trimmed.

A property that is well-cared for and shows some love and attention to detail will pay off in the end. It's the first thing a buyer will see. Make it count!

If hedges are blocking the street view to the house, remove them and consider a wrought iron fence instead. The fence will denote the boundaries of the property, but it also allows a clear view to the front of the house.

While lighting the walkway, make sure it's free from defects and cracks. With a little investment, you can replace the sidewalk and kick things up a notch. It's the little things that add to the whole experience. Buyers will appreciate them.

Be sure all sliding doors open smoothly and the handles are secure. If the sliders need a great deal of work, replace them and consider French doors, they add a great deal of light into the home, but they aren't as high maintenance as sliders.

Remember, when buyers drive by to look at the house, if they see a home that is well cared for, up-to-date, and welcoming they'll immediately get the sense that the inside must be great too. They'll want to stop and see it. First impressions really matter!

Online search and photographs.

Now that your house is ready to show to prospective buyers, you've still got one more thing on the staging list to check off. *A picture really is worth a thousand words.* Good photographs will showcase your home and make it look sensational. Using both indoor and outdoor shots gives the buyer a more complete picture of the property.

As a real estate agent for many years I've seen it all—at least 70% of the properties on-line have horrible photos of the home, and we won't even touch on the agent photos themselves!

Having great pictures of your project to post online will expedite the sale of your house. A super majority of homebuyers begin their search online, many using mobile devices in the search.

"A WHOPPING 89% OF BUYERS START THEIR SEARCH ON-LINE.
HOW YOUR HOUSE LOOKS ON-LINE IS THE MODERN
EQUIVALENT OF "CURB APPEAL"
—Barbara Corcoran

According to NAR statistics, 65 percent of people that show up at homes have seen the property online, while 38 percent set a showing after they discovered the house driving in the neighborhood. Top search parameters include the number of bedrooms and bathrooms.

If you are working with a real estate agent to sell the home, he or she will have the photos taken. This expense is covered by the listing broker's commission. Demand great photos!

If you're in a slower selling market, consider having your photographer shoot a video of the house and post it on-line at YouTube. Recently, in just one fiscal quarter, YouTube.com registered 118,000 searches for "buying a house."

Think of it this way: A buyer will see your house three times;

1. The first time he sees your home will normally be on the Internet.
2. The second time a buyer sees the house is when they drive by.
3. The third time the buyer sees the house is during a showing with a real estate agent, or open house.

Make it memorable for them. That's why staging is paramount to the sale.

Conclusion

In conclusion, craftsmanship and details are everything when flipping a residence. Purchasing a home to occupy is an emotional rather than a rational decision for many home buyers. When you know exactly what to do, it's not too difficult to really make your residential flip "pop" in the eyes of buyers. You'll have fun and make money doing it!

CHAPTER TWELVE

MARKETING YOUR PROPERTY

In this chapter I'll teach you everything you need to know to market your residential flip for a quick, high value sale. Properly marketing your refurbished flip is crucial. Once your house is perfectly and beautifully staged, you must present it for sale to the residential real estate market.

1. Have you interviewed and chosen the perfect agent to represent you?
   Your perfect agent is Internet and social media savvy, has a proven track record for selling his/her listings, and possesses ninja negotiation skills.
2. Have you determined the perfect price for your flip?
   Determining the perfect price for your flip is part skill and part art, while trusting the numbers. Your agent will calculate an estimated listing price, using listed and sold comparables.
3. Have you and your agent decided how to market your flip?
   Your agent will have multiple channels to market your flip such as the MLS, and ensuring the listing is shared in social media platforms including Zillow.com, Realtor.com, etc. Have you reviewed your agent's marketing plan, and are the activities scheduled with specific dates to ensure success?

Interviewing agents.

Having the right real estate agent listing and marketing your house can make all the difference when it comes to selling. Our goal is to get the highest amount of money, in the least amount of time, with the fewest potential problems. Finding the right agent can take some time.

According to Michael Soon Lee, the regional manager for Homes and Gardens Mason-McDuffie Real Estate in Walnut Creek, California, finding the right agent is akin to dating. "It's a long-time, intimate, trusting relationship. If it doesn't feel right at the beginning, it's probably not going to get any better." In my personal experience, it's true.

Your hope, of course, is that your first flip will be the first of many to come. Therefore, picking the right agent, someone you'd like to develop a long-term relationship with, is truly imperative. You've already interviewed and chosen the perfect agent to work with in finding homes—is he/she the correct agent to market and resell the completed flip?

Since a real estate agent only gets paid when the house is sold, obviously they should be motivated to obtain a sale. However, some agents are more motivated and more capable than others. If an agent is too busy, will he or she have time to market, show, and handle the details of selling your flip? On the other hand, the busiest agents usually have teams supporting them, which could be to your advantage.

Usually, if an agent knows that you are a serious real estate investor, there will be more incentive for them to cultivate a long-term relationship with you, because it means a potentially significant future stream of income. Just make certain that your personality and work style meshes well with your agent's and that he/she can handle the job.

Proper pricing and active marketing are truly the keys to selling your house. Ask your prospective real estate agent how he or she intends to market your house. What steps will he or she take to ensure the house's visibility? Will the agent host open houses? Will the agent personally be there or will an assistant? Will they have the house on an agent tour where other agents will see it and pass on the information to their clients? Have you reviewed examples of their marketing flyers and brochures? What type of on-line marketing is provided?

Avoid agents that are part-time or sell houses as a hobby. Real estate is a business that requires an active agent, one who is in the trenches day in and day out. Your business needs an agent with an undivided attention who has his ear to the ground, and intimately understands what is happening in the marketplace.

You don't have to hire the #1 agent—I sometimes prefer the hungry newer agent, as in the Avis #2 "We Try Harder" commercial.

The availability of your agent is critical. Be certain to ask your prospective agent about his or her availability during the interview. Do they have a team, or are they an individual agent? Do they have an assistant or are they the assistant!

The ideal agent.

Finding an agent who knows your neighborhood is great, but more important is an expert in pricing. You need someone who knows that prices may vary significantly from one block to another and from house to house, so analyzing this data and determining fair market value is critical.

INSIDER SECRET: *I've been licensed for over 25 years, and I've seen homes so far <u>underpriced</u> it should be illegal, usually by a real estate agent that knows nothing about the neighborhood or market, and the same for homes grossly <u>overpriced</u>. An experienced real estate agent will provide the numbers and the black and white data to back it up, that will help you pretty much pin-point what the selling price should be.*

YOUR FIRST FIX & FLIP

Nothing will hurt you worse in the fix and flip business than overpricing your renovated properties!

A real estate agent who is a "neighborhood expert" can be a real advantage to you because he will have an intimate knowledge of the neighborhood and contacts within the neighborhood. A neighborhood expert may have a list of clients and or potential buyers who are looking for a specific home in your neighborhood.

Nevertheless, the "neighborhood expert" is a bit overrated in our connected society. With instant access to every home listed and instant access to neighborhood statistics and data, most competent agents can nail pricing and access to potential buyers as exactly as the neighborhood expert.

An agent who possesses social media skills is a plus. He can navigate and promote your house in dozens of on-line venues that will draw attention and a potential buyer to your door. Have you viewed your agents Google+ and Facebook business page to see if there is current activity? A tech-savvy agent is a must.

Try to find an agent who has a solid history of selling 100% of their listings. The data is available to determine what percentage of an agent's listings have sold, and how close the sales price was, to the list price. This is important data to look at, especially on the agent that is recommending an exceptionally high list price.

Our goal is to get the property sold, not list it at such a high price that the agent beats us up for a price reduction every 30 days! This is the tactic of some agents.

An agent may have many talents that they bring to the sale. They may be great at marketing and showing houses. Their people skills may be exceptional. An agent may possess incredible knowledge of the market and know how to move houses. Yet, there is one attribute an agent must have above all the rest. They must be great negotiators.

The ability to negotiate is the most important skill an agent can have. An agent needs to know how to read the buyer's minds and to anticipate where the deal is going. They must know how to work the deal. A strong intuition and years of quality sales experience can help the agent when it comes time to negotiate.

Having an agent experienced in negotiations will benefit you immensely. They can tell you when you should hold tight and when you should raise or lower the sale price a bit. They can advise you in numerous ways that will give you an advantage—there are contract negotiating tactics that don't involve the price at all.

An agent who possesses all the right attributes for selling your house is a major part of your success in the flipping equation. Another factor is also necessary when it comes to the right agent. You!

When you find the real estate agent that meets all your requirements, listen to them. They know what they're doing. A full-service agent has the skills to walk you through what can be a mine field, but if you don't listen, you're tying your own hands and you'll hamstring the sale.

Assessing the property value.

THE PERFECT PRICE. Once you've settled on the perfect agent, he or she will complete a though analysis on the home to assess the value and determine the best listing price for the house.

In advance of this, your agent will do a walk through with you at which time you'll point out any updates and upgrades you've completed. The agent's completed market analysis will include homes that have sold and comparable homes in the area that are on the market. Your agent should also offer to show you any of the homes currently for sale, if you'd like to compare them personally for condition and price. It's good to understand the competition.

Naturally, your agent will recommend a price at the highest level they can for the size, type and condition of your completed fix-up house, and the neighborhood property values.

Nevertheless, if the house price is set too high, it will take longer to sell. It's important for you to understand and consider current market trends when pricing the house. Your agent will provide this information.

"NOWADAYS PEOPLE KNOW THE PRICE OF EVERYTHING
AND THE VALUE OF NOTHING."
—Oscar Wilde

Being stubborn is a great trait to have when fixing your flip. It keeps you going and helps you to get the job done correctly. Being stubborn about pricing your completed fix-up may undermine everything you set out to accomplish. If the house isn't selling because it's priced to high, the home can get market age, and potential buyers begin to wonder what's wrong with the house.

"Market Age" is not a great thing when it comes to real estate. The house may be in extraordinary condition, but potential buyers won't know that, and won't have any interest in finding out, if the price is way out of whack with other homes in the neighborhood.

I always price my homes at, or slightly below, the current market value. In highly competitive markets, pricing slightly below the market will result in multiple offers and even a bidding war. This is an excellent strategy, requiring a savvy and talented agent to successfully pull it off.

DO IT YOURSELF ESTIMATE. Looking for other sources of value vs. your real estate agent? Check out Zillow.com and their Zestimate tool. Enter your house address and see what Zestimate says.

Zestimate can adjust for the renovations you've made. Just enter in the upgrades, additions and improvements you've made. Zestimate will process the information immediately and provide you a result.

With Zestimate, you can even see the current listed comparable houses and determine the average sale price. It's simple and just one more source to estimate value.

Zillow and other on-line automated value systems will never be as accurate as a hand crafted real estate agents estimate, it's just not possible. There is no way for an automated system to take into consideration your specific neighborhood location, the improvements you've made, the condition of your home vs. others that have sold, your specific lot in reference to views and traffic, schools and highway access. Trust the professionals for the most accurate numbers.

As I mentioned earlier, a super-majority of potential home buyers start their home search online. Normally, those searches have parameters of bedrooms, bathrooms, etc., and always pricing. If you're looking for a $400,000 sale, that's fine. However, search parameters for a buyer may be $350,000 to $399,000. Set your price to fit the search parameters. People may be willing/able to pay a little more, but their searches online tend to be conservative, at least to start.

Marketing your home.

Without a proper marketing plan, your agent's phone may not ring, and neither will your doorbell (Crickets). Marketing is the quintessential tool for selling your flip. It's just as important as any tool in the tool bag.

From the beginning, before you hire your real estate agent, you need to have a good understanding about their marketing plan. Find out exactly what they plan to do in terms of marketing and when.

You understand at this point the importance of having a construction schedule and sticking to it with your fix and flip. It's just as important that your agent have a marketing plan, with dates, and they stick to it. Part of your job, being the orchestrator of your project, will be to ensure your agent follows his/her marketing proposal, meeting dates and deadlines that exceed your expectations.

The #1 site people are searching for homes on today is Zillow.com followed by Realtor.com. Look for and verify your house is available on-line and the listing details are correct.

Since your agent had a professional photographer come out and shoot photos of your renovated house, they may have created a virtual tour online. It helps give buyers the sense that they're walking through your house. They can look at each room from different perspectives and get a feel for the layout.

If you have an especially unique property with truly spectacular architecture, lot and views, think about using a drone. Locate a professional photographer using drones. They can help you showcase the property and shoot some awe-inspiring videos that will send people to your front door.

As a courtesy, speak with your real estate agent if you're interested in doing some marketing on your own. Don't overlap or intrude on the marketing your agent is conducting—they're the expert! You should be focused upon follow-up with potential sellers that have contacted you through your automated marketing efforts to find and secure your next fix and flip project.

With your own marketing efforts or contacts, what happens if you find the buyer? Do you still pay a real estate commission? These are discussions you've have to have with your real estate agent prior to signing the listing agreement.

As you're working on your project, you'll have individuals stop by frequently that are interested to know if you'll be renting the home, selling it, or moving in. If you have individuals that have expressed an interest in buying the home, list their name as an exclusion in the listing agreement. If they buy the home, you don't owe a commission.

Don't take advantage of your right to exclude sales prospects you develop on your own. Your agent is working hard for you! Your agent is your advocate, negotiating on your behalf, working night and day to sell your home and earn a commission. They don't get paid a dime unless they are successful.

The job of a real estate agent is much tougher than anyone can imagine. Brokers and agents work very hard to earn their commissions. Be grateful to them for the service they provide. A good agent is your advocate who will guide you and root for your success. Treat them right! Remember, they may bring you your next big flip!

Conclusion

In conclusion, you must possess many business skills in order to be successful at residential flipping. The hiring of professionals, negotiation, and marketing are definitely some of those skills. Agents are absolutely crucial to the process, so select your agent very carefully. Interview several prospective agents who are experts in your area. Then, continue to act as the coordinator/orchestrator to ensure your agent is marketing the home as scheduled.

CHAPTER THIRTEEN

REVIEWING OFFERS

In this chapter I will walk you through the often-complex process of receiving and reviewing offers to sell your first residential flip. What you might believe to be simple and straightforward can quickly become complicated. If your market is hot, you may find yourself juggling multiple offers. If your market is tepid, you may find yourself accepting an offer contingent upon the sale of the buyer's home.

The cycle of finding, fixing and flipping is almost complete. The demanding work is almost done. Your house is renovated, the staging is finished, the curb appeal is perfect, and potential buyers have toured your house. Now, some buyers are ready to submit their offers.

With all the energy you've expended in getting this far on your first flip, you might be tempted to take the first offer that comes through the door. However, this is an appropriate time to step back and take a breath.

Give yourself some credit for getting to this stage! It hasn't been easy, but you've hung in there. Just receiving an offer means you've succeeded in refurbishing a house that people want to buy!

Reviewing and accepting offers may seem easy, but it does take some discipline, analysis and strategy. It's a balancing act, really.

After a careful review of the offer(s), you have three options:

First—ACCEPT THE OFFER.

Let's say you received an offer that meets all your expectations. Great! If that's the case, and the closing date and financing work for you, then go for it!

INSIDER SECRET: *As a real estate broker with over 25 years of experience, I can tell you the first offer you receive is generally the best. Don't look a gift horse in the mouth. Do everything within your power to negotiate a win-win with this potential buyer.*

Second—REJECT THE OFFER.

Don't be in a rush, especially if you have multiple offers. Look over the terms of each offer. If something is extremely disagreeable to you, you should reject the offer.

What could be considered disagreeable?
- A super low-ball offer.
- An offer to purchase the home, months down the road.
- Inspection dates and deadlines that are weeks and weeks away.
- No "pre-qualification" letter from a lender.
- A contingent offer "we'll buy your home when our home sells."

Or perhaps the buyer or buyer's agent is just too demanding, and demanding too much.

Third—COUNTER OFFER OR COUNTERPROPOSAL.

This is generally the most typical scenario, even if you're countering something simple, like tightening up a date or deadline.

If you don't like the terms of the offer, but you feel that there is likely room to negotiate, then have your agent make a counter offer with terms that are more to your liking.

Counter offers or counter proposals.

After the buyer has presented the seller with a contract to purchase the house, the seller (you) may come back and want some changes on any item(s) in the contract. These changes are drawn up and presented to the buyer as a counter offer or counterproposal.

The buyer and the buyer's agent will look over the counterproposal. If the terms are agreeable, the buyer signs the counter and submits it to the seller. The deal is done.

Should the potential buyer not like the terms in the counterproposal, the buyer may submit a counter to your counterproposal listing the terms that are preferred. The seller then addresses those changes and can either agree or once again, counter the buyer's counteroffer. It's a nerve-wracking tennis match of sorts, one where emotions, if not checked, can run away with you.

The price of the house may not be the only item addressed in the counterproposal. Dates for closing, inspections, loan approval deadlines, and other issues can also be included. The inclusion or exclusion of appliances and sometimes even furniture may be listed in counterproposals.

Haggling can be difficult and, in the case of counterproposals, time consuming. Sometimes, counterproposals can become ridiculous. Your agent should have a good rapport with the buyer's agent and may be able to determine the buyer's true goal. This tactic may eliminate a few rounds of counterproposals.

How long can counterproposals continue?

If there are issues with the points in the contract, the process can continue until one or both parties are satisfied or consider it futile to continue. No legal limit is set for this process. Desire, determination, and willingness are the key factors in counterproposals.

How is a counterproposal rejected?

You might be surprised to know that in some states, whether a seller must respond or not, is dictated by statute. For example, in Colorado, a seller doesn't have to respond to a counter proposal at all. Often times a counter is ignored, just to let the buyer know its way outside of even being close to being agreeable.

Additionally, you could be shocked to learn that in some states, if your real estate agent brings you a full price offer, which you reject, you may still be liable for the broker's commission. They have done their job. Your real estate listing agent will know what the laws are in your city and state.

There are several ways for you, the seller, to reject a contract or counterproposal. You can simply ignore the offer or sign the bottom of the contract in the designated spot for rejecting the offer and initial it, if that's an option in your contract. You can also write "Rejected" across the face of the contract and initial it.

In most states, you're not obligated to put your rejection in writing at all. As a courtesy, you may direct your agent to contact the buyer's agent and notify he/her the offer has been rejected.

In buying a home, the buyer's offer is generally impacted by their individual circumstances. It's what they feel they can do *now*. As the seller, you must ascertain how to counter the offer by asking the buyer to bend a little, but you don't want them to break and walk away from the deal.

Look at the situation from your buyer's perspective. By looking at things from the buyer's point of view, you may be able to discern what they really want. The ability to find a common denominator, a target point, and a price you can both agree on may be possible without offending and losing the buyer.

Your agent can be very helpful with this strategy. If you and your agent get to know the buyer and their needs, you'll be better able to understand their position and meet their expectations without losing them.

As in any winning negotiation, both sides must feel they are getting what they want in the deal for this to be successful. Consider giving up some things on your side to achieve what you want from them. Instead of the push-pull angle, use a strategy of give and take. It will work for both sides and make the negotiations much more amicable.

When presenting the counterproposal, your real estate agent should verbally accentuate the points you like to the buyer's agent. "We like the price, we like that the buyers are well qualified…" These are the points upon which you both agree. Save the issues that don't work for last. The list of positives may outnumber the negatives making the issues you disagree upon seem fewer.

Again, price may not be your buyer's only consideration. Location may be at the top of his/her list. The buyer may need to be in your area because it makes the work commute much shorter. Your buyer's decision may hinge upon an excellent school district that serves the area. Buyers may have many different reasons they wish to buy your house, or a house in your neighborhood. By learning their needs, you can address them.

Avoiding buyer's remorse.

Once the negotiations are done and you have an accepted offer, it doesn't mean the house is sold. In a sense, you must continue to sell the house.

Purchasing a house is a huge, emotional decision for your buyers, one that naturally involves large sums of money. That super excitement of finding the ideal house and getting it under contract can quickly fade to "What was I thinking?" This is the dreaded Buyer's Remorse that inevitably comes the day after an accepted contract.

Your real estate agent and the buyer's agent can help the buyers to feel vested, not only in the house, but also in the neighborhood. As a contractor, you may have interaction with the buyers at the property, as they ask to come in and measure for window coverings, etc.

Handle the buyers with care and help them to overcome their anxiety, which can reach new levels at any stage prior to closing. You don't want them to have a sudden panic attack and completely walk away from the deal.

As you have the opportunity, continue to show them the advantages of the beautiful home they have under contract. Address any questions and issues that arise, but also pepper them with the abundant positive aspects of buying the home.

It can take some work, but in the long run, it's worth it. This home purchase may be the largest investment of their lifetime, so be patient, kind, and helpful. You'll get your flip sold, and the buyers will get the house they want.

Dates and deadlines.

Any offer you receive should have reasonable dates and deadlines for your potential buyer to act and seal the deal.

In hot markets, this is especially true. You, the seller, need a definitive "yes" or "no" so that you can move on to the next, if this isn't going to work. When you give the potential buyer too much time to think about things, the sales process can bog down and you risk losing the sale. I've seen buyers jump out of a deal, using one of the contingent dates, to purchase another home that has just come on the market! Maintain control of your contract and situation by demanding reasonable dates and deadlines.

Keep response times firm during the offer/counter offer process. With a hot market, you don't want to be tied up if the deal goes south. Buyers need to know that they must act by a given deadline or they may lose the opportunity to purchase your property, because you have other interested buyers waiting in the wings.

Multiple offers.

Receiving multiple offers to buy your residential flip is one of the best things that can happen. It's good news for you and your real estate agent. Multiple offers certainly complicate things, but it gives you power in the bargaining process.

I briefly touched on this earlier, but let's look at it more closely and see what really happens when there is more than one offer on the property.

The seller's agent and the buyer's agent typically are different agents and the bargaining and negotiation process can become complicated. The seller's agent wants the highest price, with the least potential for problems, and a quick closing. The buyer's agent wants the lowest price. Each agent is charged with doing their best for his/her client.

Real estate agents abide by a Code of Ethics which demands honesty. Agents must not make any declarations or disclosures that may not be in their client's best interest. As mentioned earlier, it significantly benefits an agent to know all they can about the potential buyer/seller. Any agent walks a fine line in providing too much of that information.

Perhaps nothing is more complicated for sellers and their agent than a multiple offer scenario. So that a potential buyer doesn't miss out on an opportunity to purchase a house that he wants, the buyer's agent needs to make certain that the buyer understands the seller of the house might receive multiple offers.

For the buyer, this means take your best shot. The buyer should name the highest price he's willing to pay for the house with his/her initial offer. They may get only one chance to buy the house. The offer must stand out. A buyer is not guaranteed the chance of a counteroffer, or the opportunity to make another offer.

By submitting a high clean offer, the potential buyer is more likely to have his offer accepted. During the home inspection contingency period, the buyer may be able to lower his original bid if the inspection turns up significant problems.

The seller is obviously looking for the best possible offer. The best possible offer might be something like a full price, all cash offer or it might be a full price offer made by a buyer who's been prequalified for a loan. If a seller receives multiple offers on his flip, he might not even need to consider counter offers. Certainly, multiple offers can speed up the entire sales process.

A buyer's agent can be authorized to tell the seller's agent that they would prefer to receive a counter offer, rather than a rejection. This conveys the message that the buyer is motivated to purchase the house and is willing to negotiate. With multiple offers, this is the second-best option to an "all cash, quick close, waive contingencies" offer.

Market trends play an integral role in selling houses. If the market is hot the seller will likely receive multiple offers. He therefore has most of the control. In a super-hot market, another tactic for a buyer is to add a "purchase price escalation addendum" which states that the buyers are willing to pay "X amount" above and beyond the highest price offered for the house, up to X amount.

Multiple offers aren't only differentiated by price. Sale terms also factor into the decision. Offers with the best price as well as terms will move to the top of the pile. For example, an all cash offer to purchase your flip that can close in 30 days would likely beat an offer to close in 90 days with a new mortgage.

Multiple offers can make a seller feel overwhelmed by choices and deadlines. Your greatest fear is that you'll accept an offer that you like, and then another offer comes in that's much better.

INSIDER SECRET: *One-way agents help buyers deal with potential multiple offers is to set a date and time to consider all offers at once. "The seller will review all offers Friday at 5:00 p.m." as an example. Your agent must stick to that date and present all offers to you on that date and time. This gives buyers' agents a set amount of time to tour the house and submit offers. It gives you the opportunity to get as many offers in your hands as possible. I've seen properties get bid way up using this tactic.*

Depending upon where you live, the process for reviewing and accepting offers may vary. In some markets the agent that has written the offer for the buyer (the buyer's agent) will present the offer to you. In other markets, your agent will review and present all offers to you for consideration. Other markets still—both agents are present.

Along with the offer you receive, a buyer's agent may attach a letter that a potential buyer has written for you to consider with your review. This could possibly disclose that the purchaser is a Veteran with a family, or maybe a person who lost their home in a fire… whatever may tug on your heart strings, to give special consideration. You may have used this strategy when you bought the flip.

How should you respond to multiple offers on a refurbished flip?
- You can simply accept the highest priced offer and close the deal.
- You can send out a counter offer to the best buyer candidate.
- You can send out multiple counter offers to the top buyers on his list (good price plus good terms) and see how they respond.
- Or you can request your agent ask for prospective buyers' best, and highest bids.

If you've chosen a savvy and experienced agent, he/she should have experience dealing with multiple offers. Follow the advice of a smart, seasoned real estate agent when making your choice of offers.

Cash is king.

When you bought your house to flip, you faced competition from other buyers. Your offer to purchase the house was accepted by the seller not only because you offered him a good price, but also because you offered the seller excellent terms.

Now you are in exactly the same situation with your potential buyer. Which buyer can really perform on the contract? Which buyer is most likely to be able to complete the sale in a reasonable amount of time? Do you have buyers who are pre-approved? If so, how much home can they afford? These are some of the questions you'll be asking when you and your agent review the offers.

Pick the offer that is clean, clear, and uncomplicated with the best financial terms. Remember, cash is king. Cash deals win out over the highest offer because there's no waiting for financing approval. You can close the sale much faster.

Not choosing a cash offer can result in a longer escrow (more time before closing), drawing out the process. If you choose to accept an offer that includes financing, you always run the risk that the property may not appraise, or the buyer's loan may ultimately be turned down for any numbers of legitimate and silly reasons. And then you have to start all over.

By accepting an all cash offer, you may wind up getting less money for your refurbished flip, but you're assured that you are going to get paid. Cash offers generally include far fewer inspections or contingencies. There's no waiting for property appraisals, loan approvals, or inspections that may never occur. There's less chance for buyer's remorse. If you accept an offer that cashes you out quickly while still giving you a reasonable profit, you're set to move on to the next flip.

Contingent offers and contingencies.

Contingent offers are contracts to purchase that provide a way for the buyer or seller to back out of the contract with little or no penalty, should the need arise.

Keep a watchful eye on contingency dates. A sophisticated buyer or his agent may try to use them as leverage to back out of the deal. Have your agent remove any verbiage that may allow your buyer to slow down the sales process or back out of the sales contract entirely.

The two most common contingencies in residential real estate are the home inspection contingency and mortgage approval contingency. Usually, no laws specifically govern these two contingencies, but your agent should be able to guide you regarding the typical customs in your area.

In my market it's customary to give a potential buyer 7-10 days to complete their physical inspection of the property, and 30 to 45 days for formal loan approval. Again, the buyer should have already provided a "pre-qualified" (lender has looked at credit, income and expenses and is confident they can get loan approval), or "pre-approved" (they are fully approved to purchase up to X amount) letter at the time they submitted their offer to you for review.

Never accept an offer that does not have a lender letter attached. Plus, your agent should talk directly with the lender prior to you accepting any offer.

If your potential buyer requests a month to complete a home inspection and 90 days for mortgage approval... run! Especially if you are new to residential real estate, allow your experienced real estate agent to guide you in these strategies.

The riskiest contract may be the "contingent contract" where the potential buyer has a home to sell and close prior to being able to close on your house. Now you have twice the potential for problems, delays, and contracts falling apart.

CONTINGENT ON SALE. The Contingent on Sale is a contingency that allows a prospective buyer to back out of his/her agreement to purchase your flip if their existing property doesn't sell. In some cases, the buyer may not even have listed the house for sale yet.

If you accept a contingent offer (and I have a few times in my 30-year career) the contingency allows you as the seller to keep marketing the home to other potential buyers. If you receive a new "better offer" you can give the contingent offer buyer 48 hours to remove the contingency or lose the ability to purchase the home. If the buyer can't remove the contingency, the contract becomes null and void.

When you accept a contingent offer, you may be able to continue marketing your home, but the listing is now considered, "Under Contract."

If your house is under contract, buyers won't be as enthusiastic about looking at it because the possibility of buying it isn't as good as with other properties. Potential buyers are far less likely to allow themselves to become emotionally invested in your flip when it's already under contract. This is a big deterrent to buyers.

In the event you're offered a sales contract with these contingencies, it doesn't mean you should avoid the deal. Nevertheless, there are some things you should evaluate if you are going to consider an offer with these contingencies. You and your agent have homework to do.

If the contingency property is listed, have your agent run comparables on it. Is it on the market? Is it priced right? How long has it been on the market? Will it sell in its current condition, over the competing competition?

How long have other houses in the area been for sale? The current market does play a huge part in all of this. If the market is soft, the buyer may not be able to sell their home in a timely manner, leaving you tied up if you've agreed to a sales contract with a contingency.

If the contingent property is Under Contract; has that buyer completed all of their inspections? Has the property appraised? Is the buyer's loan approved yet? Does that buyer have a home to sell? Etc.

Yet another factor to consider is how long your flip has been on the market. Have there been other offers? What is the feedback? What is the competition to your house? If buyers are scarce, this type of contract may work for you.

Be sure to listen to your agent's opinion on the various aspects of these contracts—chances are they've closed more deals than you, but ultimately, you decide. It's your property, you're the boss.

Always understand what the risks are if you accept a contingent offer on your flip. There's a real risk to you that the deal will not work, and your interest clock is still ticking.

Conclusion

In conclusion, reviewing offers to purchase your residential flip is as complicated as every other aspect of the process, including finding your property, purchasing it, and renovating it. If you've chosen an excellent house, renovated it well, and then marketed it with the assistance of your agent, you should expect a great offer and possibly many. It's crucial that you work closely with your agent at this time so that you can navigate every detail of the offer process. State laws relating to offers on contracts for sale vary, trust your real estate agent for expert advice.

CHAPTER FOURTEEN

CLOSING AND BEYOND

In this chapter, you will learn how to properly close your transaction and collect your proceeds, so that you can pay off the loan you used to buy your flip house, all of your subcontractors, and your taxes. I'll teach you how to get your stalled buyer's loan moving again and how to party like a professional once your profit is wired to your bank account. Finally, I'll teach you how to honestly evaluate your own performance so that you can make even more money on your next flip!

Now you can see the finish line. The closing date is set and you're ready to close your first real estate transaction and move on to your next flip! But before you move on to your next flip, you need to review the closing process and make sure you're ready.

The closing or "close of escrow" transfers ownership of the house you've just renovated to the new buyer. It's the time when all of the contractual agreements have been fulfilled.

It's a big day for both the buyer and the seller. The biggest question for both buyer and seller is: How long will the closing take?

Closing a cash deal should take less than an hour, although most home buyers will have a typical 15 or 30-year mortgage to buy a home.

Closing a non-cash deal is really dependent upon the buyer's lender and how long it takes to get all of the loan documents signed. Everyone might want a quicker closing, but each lender has required documents. Since the financial melt-down of 2008, borrowers trying to close a real estate transaction face an even bigger stack of loan documents.

The day of closing is the day all your obligations will be paid off! Any mortgage(s) you have will be paid off and the interest clock will stop running. Your real estate agent, who's worked so hard to earn his commission, will be paid. Pro-rated taxes and utilities will be collected as well as your share of the closing costs and any other contract items.

At the end of closing your net proceeds can be wired directly into your bank account. This will provide the money needed to pay any capital gains tax you may owe on the transaction. The rest is profit to be used on your next flip!

Your closing will typically be handled by a title company, although state laws and customs may vary. It may be handled by an attorney or escrow company in your state. If you've followed my advice and taken the time to find a smart, savvy, hardworking real estate agent, he/she should be able to give you some excellent guidance on this issue because they've likely handled hundreds of closings. Another excellent source of guidance on this issue would be your real estate attorney.

The company you choose will be responsible for collecting all the necessary documents and making certain that they are in order. They will also collect and disburse all monies owed and make certain that the chain of title to your first flip is clear.

When a closing takes place at a title company or an attorney's office there's usually some unbiased third party such as an escrow officer or an attorney whose job it is to ensure that the buyer and seller fulfill all promises they made to one another in the contract for sale. The seller receives the sales price for the house and the buyer receives clear title to the house. The escrow officer or attorney receives a fee for his service. If something goes wrong with the closing, he/she may be liable.

When you bought your flip, you probably had to attend the closing in person. You may have had to sign lender/mortgage documents at that time. That's what the buyer will do in this case. However, you do not need to be there.

If it works better for your schedule, you may be able to "pre-sign" the deed and other necessary closing documents prior to the actual closing. However, most title companies, attorneys, and escrow companies want the buyer and seller present for the signing. This is something that you can work out in advance.

I personally attend my closings because I like to meet the buyers, shake their hands, and build some rapport. This may be the first time I've ever met them. I'll typically leave after I've signed my side of the documents. There's no sense in sitting around for an extra hour while the buyers sign loan documents. Wish them well and go have lunch with a friend. Your proceeds will be in your bank account by the end of the day!

If you're traveling and have no choice but to use a power of attorney to sign your closing documents for you, this will have to be set up well in advance. Remember it's always a smart idea to be a "hands on" real estate investor—never be too busy to be involved in every aspect of your business. Alternatively, your escrow officer might be willing to overnight the closing documents you need to sign to your hotel. Just be aware that you'll likely have to sign them in front of a notary public. Most cities have traveling notaries today.

Never be shy or embarrassed about asking your real estate agent or escrow officer the specifics of the documents you are signing. In the beginning you may not be familiar with everything you're asked to sign and or provide… educate yourself.

Remember that it's your responsibility to supervise your real estate agent, attorney, and escrow officer when they are preparing and signing the closing documents, no matter how uncomfortable that might make you feel. Everyone makes mistakes, so read over all of your documents and ask the professionals questions.

Upon the close of escrow, your attorney or escrow officer will wire the sale proceeds to your bank account if that's your preference. In the alternative, you can receive a cashier's check. There you go! It's done.

Success – party – reward yourself.

Put the soda and champagne on ice, grab some eats, and invite your supporters and family over for the party! What an amazing, fabulous accomplishment—congratulations!

Your first successful fix and flip—you found it, fixed it, flipped it and profited! With a lot of demanding work and the help of your amazing team, you achieved something extraordinary that other people will just sit and dream about.

> *"CELEBRATE PERSONAL VICTORIES BECAUSE NO ONE ELSE UNDERSTOOD WHAT IT TOOK TO ACCOMPLISHMENT THEM."*
> —Unknown

You should be proud of your accomplishment! No doubt, you proved the naysayers who said it couldn't be done wrong. So, kick back and enjoy the party—you've earned it.

Be sure to display before and after pictures of your flip at the party. People will love seeing the changes you've made. You never know, someone at the party may know where you can find your next flip or may even want to buy your next flip. Start keeping a list of people who express an interest in buying your flips.

Word will spread among your friends and acquaintances and before you know it they may refer you to your next fix and flip. You'll be back at it again. That's the whole idea!

It's a tremendous feeling to sell your first fix and flip. Savor that feeling. After the party, there is still something that needs to be done. What is it?

INSIDER SECRET: *Part of my celebration is to reward myself—I want you to reward yourself. You've worked incredibly hard, you're going to continue to work incredibly hard, and I believe it's important to not only thank everyone around you, but to thank yourself.*

Whether it's a stock you've been drooling over, a new watch, a European vacation, a new flat screen TV, or a new car (yes, I've done that) … reward yourself!

Uncle Sam.

You guessed it. It's time to look at the taxes you'll owe on your sale/profit.

Don't panic, just be prepared. You'll need to speak with your CPA to determine what your taxes will be on the profit. It may vary depending on the type of entity that has done the flip.

If you've flipped your primary residence as your first project, you may be eligible for a tax-free sale! Under the new tax laws of 2018, homeowners who have occupied their home for 2 of the last 5 years may fit the requirements to exclude gains from taxable income. Nevertheless, check with your accountant.

A single person living in the refurbished house for 2 of the past 5 years will not owe any taxes if he/she made less than $250,000 in profit on the sale. A married couple filing a joint tax return and living in the refurbished house for 2 of the past 5 years will not owe any taxes on $500,000 in profit. As you can see, there are advantages to living in your flip for two years if that works with your lifestyle.

Check out the IRS website and see the different topics they cover regarding real estate taxes. www.irs.gov/businesses/small-businesses-self-employed/tax-tips-real-estate

You must also consider your state tax liability. Normally, state tax laws follow the Federal Tax Code. You can calculate what you must pay and factor it into your budget.

Once the taxes are paid, you can breathe a sigh of relief.

Thank you notes.

It's time to sit down and write Thank You notes. You'll want to write a brief Thank You note to the home buyer, the contractor, the designer and each member of your flip team. Don't forget the lender who helped finance your venture and your real estate agent.

Yes, it may take a bit of time to handwrite personal notes, but they will be well-received. Your team will feel appreciated and much more likely to want to help you down the road.

I THANK YOU FOR YOUR PART IN MY JOURNEY.

Consider Thank You notes an integral part of the flipping process. You didn't get where you are without help. You had a team of people who made it happen.

Letting people know how much you appreciate their help and guidance goes a long way. A heartfelt Thank You is always in order.

A look back.

The best way to make decisions about going forward is to look in the rear-view mirror to see where you started.

Are there things you did that you would change when buying your next flip?

What are they?

_____

_____

_____

Why do they stand out?

_____

_____

_____

If something didn't go as planned, was it due to a lack of research?

_____

_____

_____

This also applies to things that went right. Think about what worked, and the whys. You can make a list of things that stand out, either good or bad.

How can you improve upon your next flip?

_____

_____

_____

Have your goals changed since buying your first flip?

_____

_____

_____

If so, what are the new goals?

_____

_____

_____

Taking the time to reflect upon the journey will make your future fix and flips even more successful.

The fix and flip business is always in a state of flux. Surprises, both good and bad, enter the picture. Monday morning quarterbacking on the project will smooth the flow of your next project.

You're wiser and more seasoned now. Yet, that doesn't mean you stop learning and growing. Each successive flip will teach you and encourage you to change. Your wisdom and expertise will grow—it already has!

When we leave our comfort zones, such as when we flip houses, we have a chance to improve ourselves, not just economically, but also emotionally and mentally. Being unafraid of change and discomfort will lead us to new and better experiences. The comfort zone will return at the end of the road.

Still, don't get complacent. Being too comfortable for too long is never a good thing. It leads to inaction.

Rate yourself on a 1-10 scale of how you did on your first flip, with 10 being the optimum number in the following areas;

My time and commitment _____.

Communication with my team _____.

Meeting dates & deadlines _____.

Choice of materials and design _____.

Staying on schedule _____.

Staying within budget _____.

Dealing with surprises _____.

How well did you score?

If you had any low numbers, note why the number was low and what caused it. Was there a segment of the fix-up stage that caused this response?

_____

_____

_____

_____

_____

_____

_____

_____

If you're honest in your responses, you'll have a blueprint on how to change things on the next flip. You'll learn how to adapt quicker and be able to identify problems in advance. By going over the list, you'll be more aware of your strengths and weaknesses.

As a Certified Professional Coach (CPC) I've been trained professionally to work with individuals on analyzing their life and or business and working on areas in need of improvement.

If you have a low number in your self-analysis, what can you do to improve in that area? Do you need additional education? Is there a meditation or patience technique that would help? Maybe it's time to delegate a task that is just not your bag?

The only way you'll grow your fix-and-flip business into a fine tuned, well operating machine, is to delegate, delegate, and delegate. Remember, you're the orchestrator! Be honest and open about doing what it takes to improve those lower numbers. We've all had them.

What's next?

Following the sale of your flip, there may be a small letdown. It's normal. For over 90+ days, you have dedicated all of your energy towards achieving one goal—fixing and selling your flip for a profit.

The remedy? Find your next house as soon as possible and get back to work!

When we started on this journey, we said that flipping houses is a business. As with any business, in order to keep it running you need to recharge and get back into the game.

PAUSE TO REFLECT. What kind of house/property will you buy this time? Will you take on a more expensive house or income property, with more expensive renovations? How is your automated marketing performing? Are you tapping every resource we've discussed?

Once you've successfully completed a flip or two, look at income property opportunities. You may find less competition and more potential profit.

You're not a newbie anymore and you'll notice that with each successive flip, things get easier. That doesn't mean there won't be problems and surprises. In residential flipping, as with any business, problems and surprises are the norm. How you handle them depends upon what you've learned.

Since going through the fix and flip progression, you've experienced the good, the bad, and the ugly. You've handled the ups and downs and managed to sell your flip for a nice profit.

Use your experiences to create a foundation for the next flip. Your confidence level will be higher on the second flip. Your growth from the first flip has been remarkable. Keep moving forward! Keep growing! Keep working harder than anyone else would expect of you!

Also, build your portfolio, add some rentals, and don't forget to save some money. Invest in education and mentorship and give back to the community and to causes that move you.

Keep moving forward. Keep finding, fixing and flipping. The future you're creating for yourself and your family has no limitations!

What do you believe?

Conclusion

To conclude, even though you've successfully located, refurbished, and sold your first flip, you must still complete escrow in order to get paid. Your project management skills and persistence will serve you here just as they have before. Remember to always be cordial, professional, and polite, but ask fellow professionals questions, as necessary. Celebrate your success and share your gifts with others, including yourself. Most importantly, look back and fine tune your process. Be honest about where you are, and what modifications you can make, to put you where your dreams have you.

"THE ONLY THING STANDING BETWEEN YOU AND YOUR GOAL IS THE BULLSHIT STORY YOU KEEP TELLING YOURSELF AS TO WHY YOU CAN'T ACHIEVE IT."
—Jordan Belfort

VISIT: WWW.FIXANDFLIP.COM

You will find the latest educational material geared specific to fix and flip developers. Plus, share your thoughts on this book and your success stories.

Learn about our many resources and support;

- Free Educational Videos

- Free Forms & Worksheets

- Join our Insider Club

- Chat with fellow fix and flip developers

- Explore Coaching to Supercharge your Business & Life!